The WAY to HEAVEN

The Gospel According to John Wesley

STEVE HARPER

Previously Published as
John Wesley's Message for Today

ZONDERVAN®

ZONDERVAN.com/
AUTHORTRACKER
follow your favorite authors

The Way to Heaven
Copyright © 1983, 2003 by Steve Harper

Previously published as *John Wesley's Message for Today*

Requests for information should be addressed to:
Zondervan, *Grand Rapids, Michigan 49530*

Library of Congress Cataloging-in-Publication Data

Harper, Steve.
    The way to heaven : the gospel according to John Wesley / Steve
Harper.—2nd ed.
        p. cm.
    Rev. ed. of: John Wesley's message for today. c1983.
Includes bibliographical references.
    ISBN-10: 0-310-25260-1
    ISBN-13: 978-0-310-25260-3
    1. Wesley, John, 1703-1791. I. Harper, Steve. John Wesley's message for today.
II. Title.
BX8495.W5H32   2003
230'.7'092—dc21

                                                    2003008390

Interior design by Todd Sprague

Printed in the United States of America

13 14 15 16   QG 6 5 4 3 2 1

CONTENTS

CONTENTS

PREFACE

People everywhere have a deep hunger for heaven. Since I wrote *John Wesley's Message for Today* in 1983, the public expression of that hunger has increased and found many new expressions, both inside and outside the Christian faith. Evidence spans the spectrum from formal theologies about universalism to ultraconservative beliefs concerning the end times. We have seen a fascination with angels, spiritism and metaphysics, visitors from outer space, the occult, and daily doses of heavenly messages carried on cable television and through the multibillion dollar "religion industry." A country-and-western song even pointed to this hunger in the lyric, "Everybody wants to go to heaven, but nobody wants to die."

But the most profound hunger for heaven is the one we find in our own hearts. We cannot escape or deny our quest for eternal life. Untold numbers of people fear that death is the end of life as we know it, and they seek some evidence that the grave does not have the last word. And even more than that, we hunger for heaven because we believe that if it is real, it should have some beneficial effect on our lives here on earth.

For these reasons, I have chosen to revise my earlier book and title it *The Way to Heaven*. There's no doubt that this is a legitimate way to organize theology, and those who are familiar with John Wesley will immediately recognize that he used this view in his own understanding of the gospel. For some time now, Wesleyan scholars have known that John Wesley was not fundamentally a conceptual theologian. He did not organize his beliefs into topics. Rather, he developed theology in relation to life. This has caused some critics to deny that he was a theologian at all, but his choice of theology as "an order of salvation" was deliberate and decisive. For him, the grand notion of redemption was summarized in the phrase "the way to heaven." His own words say it best:

> I want to know one thing—the way to heaven; how to land safe on that happy shore. God Himself has condescended to teach the way; for this very end He came from heaven. He hath written it down in a book. O give me that book! at any price, give me the book of God! I have it: here is knowledge enough for me.[1]

As we will see, understanding the gospel as "the way to heaven" allows God's sovereignty to remain supreme while at the same time inviting us on a journey that responds to grace all the days of our lives. It is theology for living—"practical divinity," Wesley liked to call it. It is a way of viewing theology that transcends Wesley's time and addresses us today. This kind of theology is more than content—it is a summons, an invitation to life.

I am grateful that Zondervan has seen fit to ask me to revise *John Wesley's Message for Today*. I never imagined that the little book would be in print for twenty years, much less having a second life beyond that. I thank Stan Gundry (who approved the original volume in 1983, as well as this one) and Dirk

---

[1]Thomas Jackson, ed., *The Works of John Wesley* (Grand Rapids: Baker, 1979, reprint edition), 5:3.

Buursma (the editor who worked with me on this edition) for supporting this revision and helping me in the preparation of it. I am equally happy that this revision appears in the 300th anniversary year of Wesley's birth.

If you have previously read *John Wesley's Message for Today*, you will quickly see that this new volume is mainly an expansion, with new chapters and only a few minor changes to the original text. You will also see that the expansion is primarily in terms of Wesley's method and mission. In 1983, I did not see the connection between his message and these additional elements as clearly as I do today. In fact, I have come to realize that we cannot properly understand his theology apart from the vision that inspired it and the purpose to which it was addressed. I trust this will become clear in what you are about to read.

As in 1983, I remain indebted to my foundational mentors Ed Robb, Frank Baker, and Albert Outler. Since then, I have been helped to see Wesley better by such friends and mentors as Paul Chilcote, Randy Maddox, Richard Heitzenrater, Ted Runyan, Ted Campbell, Robert Tuttle, Kenneth Kinghorn, George Hunter, and Howard Snyder—to name only a few. The revised bibliography at the end of the book will further reveal my sources, as will some of the endnotes. You can use these pointers to extend your study beyond this little book, which I surely hope you will do.

But most of all, the ensuing twenty years from the first edition to this one have given me two more decades of experiencing Jeannie's love and support. She has been, and continues to be, my most cherished companion on "the way to heaven." And I dedicate this new edition to her.

Blessings!
Steve Harper

A Word about Referencing

In 1983, I chose to use the Thomas Jackson edition of *The Works of John Wesley* (reprinted by Baker, 1979) as the main source for citing original references. For matters of consistency in this second edition, I have chosen to do the same.

However, I would strongly commend your use of *The Bicentennial Edition of the Works of John Wesley* (Abingdon, 1984). Many of the planned volumes are yet to appear, but this edition is superior to any previous set of Wesley's writings. To the extent that you can use this new edition, your knowledge of Wesley and your appreciation of him will grow. I have tried to reference original sources in a way that will enable you to find them easily in this edition.

I would also call your attention to the Curnock edition of Wesley's *Journal*, the Sugden edition of his *Standard Sermons*, and the Telford edition of his *Letters*. These older works were, in their day, what the new bicentennial edition seeks to be in our time. They are valuable in giving us the "historical" sense of Wesley's life and work. All of these resources are cited in the bibliography at the end of the book.

Chapter One

A PILGRIM
ON THE WAY

*Wesley offers a treasure to
the church of tomorrow
that will leave it poorer if ignored.*

ALBERT OUTLER

When you meet John Wesley, you meet someone who understands you. When you get to know him, you feel as though you've known him all your life. In the same way that you are on a journey to know God and to live for Christ, you find that he is also a pilgrim on the Way. This makes a study of Wesley much more than an intellectual pursuit or an academic assignment. It is a conjoining of minds, hearts, and spirits. It is a sharing of resolve to live life for the glory of God.

For many of us, understanding theology as a "way to heaven" is a new way to look at it. Many of us were taught to understand theology in a topical fashion, moving from subject to subject. And we were almost surely taught to study theology with little or no understanding of the person who wrote the theology in the first place. On both accounts, we make a mistake if we try to study Wesley this way.

For one thing, he was not a topical theologian. While we find every customary doctrine in his writings, we do not find them organized by topics or chapters. Instead, we discover a pilgrimage motif—theology interpreted in relation to the story of God's grace and in relation to our experience of this grace as we move through the days of our lives. And for another thing, we cannot understand the message apart from the messenger. Wesley's theology flows from his own life and experience of God. So, in this first chapter, we ask, "Who is John Wesley? What difference will it make in our Christian lives to come to know him and the message that comes to us through him?"

On the biographical level it is helpful to mention some basic facts.[2] John Wesley was born on 17 June 1703, the fifteenth child and second surviving son of Samuel and Susanna Wesley. His early life in Epworth, England, was largely shaped by the example of his parents and in particular the educational program Susanna operated in the rectory.

When he was six, he was rescued from the burning rectory in so remarkable a fashion that Susanna believed the hand of God was upon him in a special way. Accordingly, she felt a particular responsibility to nurture the life of her son. What she did had its lifelong effects. And even today John Wesley's life at Epworth is rightly considered the "cradle of Methodism."[3]

In 1713 Wesley moved to London to attend Charterhouse School. In comparison to other periods in his life, his years at Charterhouse were of lesser significance. However, while there he continued to read his Bible and say his prayers daily.[4] After six years at Charterhouse he matriculated to Christ Church College at Oxford, where he received the Bachelor of Arts degree in 1726.

Wesley's early Oxford years saw the beginning of his spiritual pilgrimage. In 1725, after reading Jeremy Taylor's *Holy Living* and Thomas à Kempis's *The Imitation of Christ,* he resolved to dedicate his life to God.[5] The next thirteen years were an agonizing attempt to work out the implications of that resolution. However, it all came together in the now-famous Aldersgate experience on 24 May 1738. There Wesley found the personal assurance necessary to give life and power to his faith.

---

[2]If you haven't yet done so, it would be helpful to read a biography of Wesley. Two recent ones are Stanley Ayling's *John Wesley* (Cleveland: William Collins Publishers, 1979) and Robert Tuttle's *John Wesley: His Life and Theology* (Grand Rapids: Zondervan, 1978).

[3]Martin Schmidt, *John Wesley: A Theological Biography* (Nashville: Abingdon, 1962), 1:63.

[4]Jackson, *Works,* 1:98.

[5]Jackson, *Works,* 11:366–67.

From that point onward Wesley became England's greatest preacher and organizer; multitudes responded to his preaching, and he sought to nurture them through the united societies, which he organized. The last sixty years of his life were a constant motion of traveling and preaching that took him over 250,000 miles (mostly on horseback) and gave him the opportunity of preaching more than 44,000 times. Erwin Paul Rudolph has observed, "In Wesley's work we see the figure of a great preacher, an untiring worker, and a popular but autocratic leader. He reveals a mind that is shrewd, but capable of humor, and that is filled with the sense of divine mission."[6]

Wesley rested from his labors on 2 March 1791. His last words served not only to capture the quality of life he lived but also the kind of life he wished for others. He died saying, "The best of all is, God is with us!"

While these facts are important, they do not fully capture Wesley, the man. There are other qualities we should be familiar with if we are to meet John Wesley in these opening pages. For me, the most appealing thing about him is that he is a fellow pilgrim in the faith. He was in search of vital faith, just as we are. When you read his diary, journal, and letters, this comes through loud and clear. He faced struggles similar to ours. He made his share of mistakes. He asked questions during times of doubt and depression. He knew the elation of victory. In a very real sense, Wesley was one of us.

Furthermore, Wesley was a *practical theologian*. This doesn't mean he was unfamiliar with theology on a scholarly level, or that he could not handle himself with the so-called theological heavyweights of his day. One reading of his *Appeals to Men of Reason and Religion* is sufficient to dispel this notion.[7] What it

---

[6]Erwin P. Rudolph, *The John Wesley Treasury* (Wheaton, Ill.: Victor, 1979), 11.
[7]Jackson, *Works*, 8:3–247.

does mean is that Wesley was primarily concerned about developing a faith that worked in everyday living. He was in search of a "scriptural Christianity" that was confirmed by human experience. The fact that his theology is biblical gives it a timelessness; the fact that it is confirmed by experience gives it an authenticity that theology in the ivory tower sometimes lacks. Wesley's theology has been road tested, and found effective.

To know Wesley is also to know a person of intense and meaningful discipline. Every day counted; every moment was a "God moment." Consequently, he gave himself daily to the spiritual disciplines of prayer, Bible study, and devotion. But discipline was never an end in itself. It was the means to a vital relationship with God and the resulting power that comes from that relationship.

As the Methodist movement began to grow, Wesley sought to instill this same spirit of discipline into his followers. The bands, classes, and societies were all organized on explicit disciplinary principles.[8] Members were held accountable for living up to the disciplines. And through the sense of personal and corporate discipline, early Methodism had both a vitality and a stability that contemporary church life sometimes fails to exhibit. To know Wesley is to know one who echoes the saying, "The soul and the body make the man; and the spirit and discipline make a Christian."[9]

As you read this book, keep in mind the word *daily*. Wesley's life and theology pulsate with this word. For over sixty years he faithfully engaged in devotional *living*. He calls us to do the same. He challenges us to break out of any compartmentalized concept of Christianity. Jesus is Lord! Every moment is to be lived in his presence. While we won't exactly match his methods, we should strive to imitate his discipline.

---

[8]Jackson, *Works*, 7:248–388.
[9]Jackson, *Works*, 13:101.

Knowing John Wesley requires that we see him in a community sense. Wesley was a churchman in the highest and best sense of the term. It's important that we see this early in this book. Too often he is cast in the light of a malcontent just looking for a good reason to start a new church. Never forget that he lived *and died* an Anglican. He did not inaugurate a new denomination, and he discouraged his followers from doing so.[10] In the very first annual conference that Wesley held in 1744, he declared his allegiance to the Anglican Church and exhorted the Methodists to constant attendance of "both the word preached and the sacraments administered therein."[11] And throughout his lifetime, Methodism was a renewal movement within the larger Anglican Church.[12]

Having said this, it is equally important to stress that Wesley's ultimate loyalty was to God. As much as he loved the Anglican Church, he loved God more. Where he felt the church had strayed, he stood against it. He was a true "son of the Reformation." The point to be stressed is that his disagreements with the Church of England were not institutional, they were scriptural. He felt that eighteenth-century Anglicanism had drifted from important scriptural norms,[13] and he viewed the Methodist movement as simply describing "the plain, old religion of the Church of England."[14] His goal was not defection, but rather renewal. His constant prayer was that the renewal could take place *within* Anglicanism. That it did not is a fact of church history, not a fact by Wesley's design. To know Wesley is to know a churchman.

---

[10]The issue here is complex. The best interpretation I've found is Frank Baker's *John Wesley and the Church of England* (Nashville: Abingdon, 1970).

[11]Jackson, *Works*, 8:280.

[12]More will be said on Wesley's theology of the church in chapter 9.

[13]For example, justification by faith, new birth, repentance in believers, entire sanctification.

[14]Jackson, *Works*, 1:232.

Because his churchmanship was based on Scripture rather than on contemporary doctrinal formulations,[15] his theology has a dynamism. He abhorred stagnant orthodoxy.[16] He sought a scriptural Christianity energized by the ongoing presence of the Holy Spirit. While his theology comes from the eighteenth century, it is not bound by it. Furthermore, it moves in harmony with Christian experience. In his preface to the Standard Sermons, he wrote, "I want to know one thing—the way to heaven."[17] For Wesley, that "way" was dynamic, *moving* from sin to glorification. In this book I have tried to capture this feature of Wesley's theology by basing the chapters on the "order of salvation" that emerges in his writings. Wesley never produced a systematic theology in the formal sense, but what he did produce is systematic and consistent. My goal is that the organization of this book will help you know Wesley in that light.

Finally, to know Wesley is to know someone you can read and understand. By his own design he avoided complex theological terminology. He wrote, "I desire plain truth for plain people; therefore, of set purpose, I abstain from all nice and philosophical speculations."[18] As previously noted, he could deal with theology on a sophisticated level when needed. But in the general course of his ministry he desired to communicate with ordinary people in understandable ways. If you've previously shied away from reading theology, you're in for a pleasant surprise in Wesley. His simplicity will not insult your intelligence, it will increase it. His life-centeredness will touch you

---

[15]Wesley fully accepted and took seriously the Anglican *Articles of Religion* and the *Homilies*. In fact, he considered them more authoritative than some of his contemporaries did. But he did so on the basis of his conviction that they were reflections of scriptural truth.

[16]Jackson, *Works*, 5:78.

[17]John Wesley, *Forty-four Sermons* (London: Epworth, 1944), vi (cf. Jackson, *Works*, 5:3).

[18]Jackson, *Works*, 5:2.

where you live and cause you to consider your own beliefs and actions. This is the kind of experience I hope you will have as you read this book. It is the kind of experience Wesley would wish for you.

I trust that this chapter has helped you sense something of a kinship with John Wesley. Such a kinship will enrich your reading of the following pages. In fact, the following chapters cannot be read in a detached manner. Wesley would not only want you to understand his message, he would want you to be affected by it. He would want you to experience the Christ to whom it points. Time and time again Wesley wrote that he "offered Christ." Through this reconstruction of Wesley's message, he is offering Christ to you yet again!

Questions for Reflection and Discussion

1. Does your experience confirm (or deny) the author's assertion that even people in the Wesleyan tradition do not know Wesley very well? If you are not in the Wesleyan tradition, how well do people in your tradition know him?
2. Among the various features of Wesley's life and theology, which is the most attractive to you? Why?
3. What are your desires and dreams as you begin this book? What do you hope it will do for you?

For Further Reading

Outler, Albert. *John Wesley.* New York: Oxford Univ. Press, 1964; reprint edition, 1981.

Wood, Skevington. *John Wesley, The Burning Heart.* Kansas City, Mo.: Beacon Hill, 1977.

Chapter Two

THE ROOT OF
THE PROBLEM
(ORIGINAL SIN)

*The doctrine of universal sinfulness,
concludes Wesley, constitutes the fundamental
difference between Christianity and Heathenism.*

MARTIN SCHMIDT

You don't have to be a Christian to realize that something is wrong with the human race. Our most brilliant social analysts stand amazed in the presence of radical, often unpredictable experiences of man's inhumanity to man. Politicians all over the world are calling for the upholding of basic human rights. All the while an ominous nuclear cloud hangs overhead, reminding us that the entire destruction of this planet is possible. Everyone seems to be asking, "What is wrong?"

When John Wesley looked at his century, he asked the same question. He understood the original creation to have been good (see Genesis 1:31)—the result of an all-loving God expressing that love through everything that was made. The opening pages of the Bible clearly show that God made a beautiful world, one that would reflect God's glory and serve God's purposes. But, in fact, this was not the world Wesley saw around him or experienced within himself. Something had gone radically wrong.

He concluded that the fundamental problem was *human sinfulness*. Interestingly, this side of Wesley is often overshadowed by his emphasis on love. While it is true that he stressed God's love as a major plank in his theology, it's also true that he was aware of the dangers of emphasizing love to the neglect of other things. In a letter to Joseph Cownley Wesley made the point clear:

> Is it not most pleasing to me as well as to you to be always preaching of the love of God? . . . But yet it would be utterly wrong and unscriptural to preach of nothing

else. . . . The bulk of our hearers must be purged before they are fed; else we only feed the disease. Beware of all honey. It is the best extreme, but it is an extreme.[19]

This statement makes it clear that Wesley's theology of love was not sentimentalism. It was love based on at least two primary considerations. First, Wesley believed that God loved man as the supreme object of his creation. Wesley believed in the original righteousness of man.[20] He expressed this belief using the words of Thomas Boston: "With the same breath that God breathed into him a living soul, he breathed into him a righteous soul. This righteousness was the conformity of all the faculties and powers of his soul to the moral law."[21] A belief in original righteousness gave Wesley his primary reason to believe in God's love.

Furthermore, original righteousness explained why people have to be saved—why redemption is the only option. Redemption only makes sense if there is prior value. If something is worthless, it can be thrown away and replaced. But if it has prior value, it must be found and restored. Redemption means that people have prior value (eternal value), and God's love will not permit anyone to be discarded. In Wesley's theology, original righteousness precedes original sin; otherwise, salvation makes no sense. As the hymn puts it, God's love is a love "that will not let us go."

But secondly, God's love was love expressed in the midst of human sin. In his *Explanatory Notes Upon the New Testament,* Wesley affirmed the universality of sin in relation to human nature, temper, and action.[22] No part of man's existence escaped

---

[19]John Telford, ed., *The Letters of John Wesley* (London: Epworth, 1931), 3:34.

[20]Jackson, *Works,* 9:339–53; 435.

[21]Jackson, *Works,* 6:435. Wesley is quoting from Boston's *Human Nature in Its Fourfold State.*

[22]John Wesley, *Explanatory Notes Upon the New Testament* (Grand Rapids: Baker, 1987, reprint edition), 530 (note on Romans 3:23).

the contamination. This view gave Wesley's theology of love an authentic substance. It was love offered in the face of rejection. It was not love expressed in the hope of getting something in return,[23] rather it was love expressed where rebellion and even hatred seemed to have won the day.

So the first step in understanding Wesley is to understand the presence of God's love in relation to the depth of human sin. Sin has struck at the root of God's intention for the human race. Consequently, there is nothing more important than confronting sin as the enemy it always is. Thus, the whole shape of Wesley's theology is an "order of salvation." It is the story of how grace operates to overcome sin and to restore original righteousness.

Wesley said it himself, "We know no gospel without salvation from sin."[24] Such a serious view of sin must be reckoned with in an age when some theologians are inclined to paint a picture of love that minimizes or ignores the fact of universal human sinfulness. Wesley cannot be read or interpreted in this light. His proclamation of great love must always be seen against the backdrop of deep need.

But what is sin? Again we must pause to get our bearings. For Wesley, sin was not some mysterious spiritual entity that attached itself to human nature like a barnacle attaches itself to the hull of a ship. Instead, Wesley spoke of sin in relational terms. His classic definition is that sin is "every voluntary breach of the law of love."[25] At its base, sin is *broken relationship,* whether that brokenness is expressed toward others or toward God. And it is important to note that the breach is conscious and willful. For Wesley, sin is not something that sneaks up on you; it arises out of you.

---

[23]This is the basis on which most human love is founded. The amazing thing about God's love is that it is offered with no strings attached. God loves even when no love is returned!

[24]Telford, *Letters,* 6:327.

[25]Telford, *Letters,* 6:322.

The result of sin is sickness. One of Wesley's favorite terms is *corruption*. Because of sin, humanity is sick unto death. Wesley's definition of sin involves a cause-and-effect relationship. The cause is willful transgression, the result is sickness. And the disease of sin has "spread itself over the whole man, leaving no part uninfected."[26] This means that sin goes deeper than any acts we commit. The Bible does not say we are sinners because we commit acts of sin; it says we commit acts of sin because we are sinners. Sin has struck at the root of what it means to be human.

Wesley believed that Adam was in a perfect state before the Fall. He bore the image of God completely, as God had intended it to be borne. But in the Fall something happened. The *imago Dei* was *radically* damaged. The moral aspects of the image were lost.[27] The natural aspects of the image were extensively marred but not completely destroyed. Humanity retained some degree of rationality, emotion, and will, but because these aspects were severely tainted, they served to increase the overall curse. Man was unable to come to God using these faculties alone. In short, the life of God in the soul of man was virtually extinguished. Wesley put it this way: "The glory departed from him."[28] Intimacy between God and man was gone. Separation was the result. Spiritual sickness unto death was the condition.

This cuts across the grain of much thinking today. Some in our society deny the objective reality of sin altogether. Others try to explain it philosophically as the absence of goodness. More often the idea itself is softened under the term *mistake* or the phrase *nobody's perfect*. So it may well be that this kind of view will take some getting used to. But it did in Wesley's day,

---

[26]Wesley, *Explanatory Notes*, 540 (note on Romans 6:6).

[27]Wesley included righteousness and true holiness in his understanding of the moral image.

[28]Jackson, *Works*, 6:272 (sermon: "The End of Christ's Coming").

too. He wrote, "It is now quite unfashionable to say anything to the disparagement of human nature."[29]

However, the eighteenth century's naive optimism did not prevent Wesley from proclaiming the picture as he saw it. It must not stop us either. We need a fresh affirmation of the reality and danger of sin, not from the standpoint of pessimism, but from the perspective of realism. For, you see, we need a Savior only if we need saving; we need a Savior only if we cannot save ourselves. This is precisely what Wesley, in his doctrine of sin, calls us to acknowledge.

Wesley drove his point home even deeper by stressing the *universality* of sin. He not only spoke of sin's nature, he also made it clear that everyone has been infected. *All* have sinned. He did not try to spell out how we share in Adam's original sin; he simply said that in some way we all died in Adam.[30] For evidence he turned not to speculation but to human conduct.

Even here Wesley was not content to point his finger at the "gross sinners" whom everyone would recognize to be such. He called on decent people to repent and be saved. He knew that one might live an outwardly respectable life and still be lost. Anyone, gross or respectable, who lived as though God did not matter, illustrated the universality of sin. This kind of sin runs silent and deep. It takes no holidays. It leaves no one immune. One of Wesley's favorite texts was Genesis 6:5, which speaks about man's heart being *continually* set on evil. In more poetic fashion, his brother Charles described this as humanity's "bent to sinning."[31]

What are the implications of this doctrine? Simply this: If sin were a "thing," we might find some way to rid ourselves of

---

[29]Jackson, *Works*, 6:55 (sermon: "Original Sin").
[30]Jackson, *Works*, 6:68 (sermon: "The New Birth").
[31]Taken from Charles Wesley's hymn "Love Divine, All Loves Excelling."

it or cut it off. But because it is an infection of our humanity, the only option is *transformation*. We cannot try hard enough, learn enough, worship enough, or work enough to heal ourselves. Outside help is the only possible solution.

I read about a man who went into the desert to live as a hermit. He reasoned that by doing so he could remove himself from this sinful world. But he didn't stay long, and when he returned, he said, "I could not run away from sin, because it was in me. Everywhere I went, there it was." I heard, too, of a woman who frantically approached an airline ticket counter, placed several hundred dollars on the counter, and said, "Use this, and send me anywhere you can and back in three days. I cannot stand it here another minute."

We eventually come to see that the problem of sin is a problem infecting the very nature of what it means to be human. Any attempts to remove ourselves from it are only exercises in futility. The solution is transformation, not escape. Wesley can help us see the futility of our efforts to treat sin as a "thing." He can help us by reminding us that, at its heart, *sin is disease*. Healing is the only solution.

This is the nature of sin in Wesley's theology. It is only natural to assume that anything this pervasive would have certain effects. Wesley spoke to some of these effects in his writings. For one thing, he said that sin makes us *dead toward God*. He spoke of the Fall as having brought death to the soul.[32] The irony of this soul-death is that it gives a false sense of security and peace. Wesley put it this way: "The poor unawakened sinner has no knowledge of himself. He knows not that he is a fallen spirit. Full of diseases as he is, he fancies himself in perfect health."[33]

[32]Jackson, *Works*, 5:54 (sermon: "Justification by Faith").
[33]Jackson, *Works*, 5:26 (sermon: "Awake, Thou That Sleepest").

Even more dangerous is that soul-death is a very active state. Wesley compared spiritual death to the branches that spring out of an evil root. The branches produce the fruit of unbelief, independence, pride, vanity, ambition, covetousness, lust, anger, envy, and sorrow.[34] Wesley went on to say that this condition, if left untreated, would evolve into eternal death.

Another effect of sin is *self-captivity*. For Wesley this was the logical consequence of being dead to God. If one is truly dead to God, then the only alternative is to turn inward and make self a god. Wesley saw humanity doing just that—and doing it in the name of freedom. Ironically this so-called freedom was the worst form of slavery. Needing a perspective on life greater than his own, man was trapped by the limits of his own reason. Needing a power beyond himself, he found himself prey to his own weakness. As someone put it, "I may be the captain of my soul, but I keep driving myself around in circles."

A third effect of sin is *helplessness to change*. Even though Wesley did not believe in the total destruction of the image of God, he did believe it had been rendered powerless to revitalize itself. Even a person under conviction was in need of grace to find victory. Wesley described this dilemma by saying, "Now he truly desires to break loose from sin and begins to struggle with it. But though he strive with all his might, he cannot conquer; sin is mightier than he."[35]

I have always been fascinated with those who call Christianity a crutch or who claim it is only for weak people. They would opt for an unrealistic optimism in human ability—a bootstrap theology, or self-helpism. If such a person were to approach Wesley and say, "Christianity is for weak people," he would reply, "Correct!

---

[34]Jackson, *Works,* 5:82–84 (sermon: "The Way to the Kingdom").
[35]Jackson, *Works,* 5:104 (sermon: "The Spirit of Bondage and the Spirit of Adoption").

And we are all weak!" We cannot pull ourselves up by our own bootstraps. Grace is essential.

It is at this very point that Wesley's theology of sin evolves into the proclamation of the Good News. He never spoke of sin's nature or its effects without also speaking of the remedy. There is power for the powerless. There is help for the helpless. There is a cure for the disease. One of his favorite texts was "Here is a trustworthy saying that deserves full acceptance: Christ Jesus came into the world to save sinners" (1 Timothy 1:15). God took the initiative. He sought us. He provided the healing medicine. In the following chapters we will see how God effects that healing. For now it is enough to know that in Christ there is deliverance and healing.

This has not been an easy chapter to write; by today's standards it seems pessimistic. But that's only because the contemporary view of man is overly optimistic. By ignoring a biblical view of sin, we have failed to come to grips with the reality and extent of sin. Wesley's view was not meant to depress people or to send them on guilt trips. Rather, it was meant to awaken them—to bring them to a realistic awareness of their condition. He felt that only then could a person adequately deal with sin. Wesley attacks expressions of self-sufficiency in order that we may fall back on the necessity of God's grace. Wesley's last word is one of hope, victory, and triumph.

Charles Wesley captured the theme of triumph over sin in his classic hymn "And Can It Be." Through these words we may hear the very voice of God:

> Long my imprisoned spirit lay
> Fast bound in sin and nature's night.
> Thine eye diffused a quickening ray;

I woke—the dungeon flamed with light!
My chains fell off, my heart was free,
I rose, went forth, and followed thee!

Questions for Reflection and Discussion

1. What evidence do you see in contemporary living that we have sentimentalized love?
2. How do you see the universality of sin illustrated today?
3. What can Wesley's view of sin offer those who are tempted to despair over the condition of their lives?
4. Think of your own experience. In what ways did God take the initiative to bring you to acknowledge your helplessness?

For Further Reading

Sermon: "Original Sin," in Jackson's *The Works of John Wesley*, 6:54–64.

Sermon: "On the Fall of Man," in Jackson's *The Works of John Wesley*, 6:215–24.

Sermon: "The Way to the Kingdom," in Jackson's *The Works of John Wesley*, 5:76–86.

Chapter Three

THE POWER TO BEGIN
(PREVENIENT GRACE)

---

*Wesley's theological system builds
on the doctrine of original sin
and prevenient grace.*

ROBERT TUTTLE

The way to heaven is a journey in which we respond to grace all along the way. It is a way that begins the moment of our conception and continues beyond the moment of our death. It is a way we did not invent, and one we cannot fulfill by our own efforts. The way must be enabled by God's prior and sustained action in our lives. It must have a starting point. For Wesley, the starting point was called *prevenient grace*.

If an artist were to paint a picture of John Wesley's doctrine of prevenient grace, he would portray a person hopelessly lost at sea. He would capture the struggle and agony on the face of the person. He would show the utter despair of the situation. The painting would carry this unwritten message: "There is nothing this man can do to save himself. Outside help is his only hope."

At this point the artist would have a problem. He would be faced with the task of adding another dimension to the work. He would have to find a way to include the presence and reality of that outside help. To be true to Wesley, he would have to show that God has broken through into the hopelessness. In theological terms, he would have to portray the idea of *prevenient grace*.

For many the idea of prevenient grace is a new idea. Even some in the Wesleyan tradition are not familiar with the term. But it is a crucial concept for understanding Wesley's order of salvation. Failure to factor it in has led some to erroneously conclude that Wesley believed in natural human ability and

complete freedom of the will. But as we shall see, that is not
Wesley's position.

Before we look at prevenient grace in particular, I believe it
is important to speak of grace in general. Grace is grace. You do
not have one kind of grace for one situation and another kind
for some other situation. By the same token God does not give
his grace in bits and pieces. We define grace in different ways
because of how we experience the grace on our end of the relationship. Grace comes to us at different stages in our spiritual
pilgrimage, and it accomplishes different effects and evokes
different responses. *But it is all grace.*

When Wesley spoke of *prevenient grace,* he meant the
grace of God that operates before our experience of conversion.[36] It is his term for the grace of God that is active before
we give conscious thought to God or to our need of him. To
use biblical language, it is the grace that comes while we are
"still sinners" (Romans 5:8). In Wesley's theology, this action
of grace is particularly important, and we need to work
through it carefully.

We must begin with the definition alluded to in the previous
paragraph. Literally, *prevenient grace* means "the grace that
comes before."[37] Before what? Before any *conscious* personal
experience of divine grace. Through his doctrine of prevenient
grace, Wesley was saying that the first move is God's, not man's.
Without this, Wesley said, we might have some room for boast-
ing. Prevenient grace removes "all imagination of merit from
man."[38] But even more to the point is the impossibility of man
to come to God on his own. Wesley stated it plainly: "It is not
possible for men to do anything well till God raises them from

---

[36]Jackson, *Works,* 6:511–13 (sermon: "On Working Out Our Own Salvation").

[37]John Lawson, *Introduction to Christian Doctrine* (Wilmore, Ky.: Asbury, 1980),
214.

[38]Jackson, *Works,* 6:508.

the dead. . . . It is impossible for us to come out of our sins, yea, or to make the least motion toward it, till He who hath all power in heaven and earth call our dead souls into life."[39]

This should lay to rest once and for all any notions that Wesley believed in natural human ability. He said it plainly: "All men are by nature not only sick, but 'dead in trespasses and sins.'"[40] The doctrine of prevenient grace means that God takes the first step to redeem humanity. And for Wesley, God allows this grace to operate in and through the human conscience.

He disliked the term *natural conscience,* which was used in his day. He believed that, while every man had a conscience, it was placed there as a supernatural gift of God.[41] His favorite text to illustrate this truth was John 1:9, where the preincarnate Word of God is said to be "the true light that gives light to every man." Clearly Wesley saw prevenient grace as the activity of God before conversion, totally apart from man's ability or initiative.

Additionally, prevenient grace is "leading grace." It is the operation of God that moves us to the place of repentance. Wesley indicated three ways in which prevenient grace "leads" us. First, it creates in us our first sensitivity to God's will; second, it produces a slight, even transient conviction of having violated his will; and third, it causes our first wish to please God.[42] Through these experiences Wesley believed a person would be led to the place of repentance, which was itself a step along the way to full salvation.

It is important to emphasize that prevenient grace is not sufficient for salvation. If a person chooses to ignore or suppress this grace, he will experience hardness of heart, with the result

---

[39]Jackson, *Works,* 6:511.
[40]Jackson, *Works,* 6:511.
[41]Jackson, *Works,* 6:509.
[42]Jackson, *Works,* 6:509.

that these stirrings of God will go unheeded. Nevertheless, because prevenient grace is involved in moving a person to the place of repentance, Wesley included it in his overall scheme of salvation. All the while he was giving priority to the activity of God. He put it this way: "God worketh in you; therefore you can work. Otherwise it would be impossible."[43] Like all other aspects of grace, prevenient grace is a gift.

In this light, two other facts emerge. First, it is grace *for all*. No one is excluded from the operation of prevenient grace. Wesley would echo the apostle Peter, who said that God is "not wanting anyone to perish, but everyone to come to repentance" (2 Peter 3:9). Second, it is grace *in all*. It is only because of grace that anything resembling the image of God remains in us. Were it not for grace we would have been stripped of anything good, noble, just, or pure. This means that we do not merely live in an atmosphere of grace; the life we now live is *due to* the grace of God!

This is Wesley's doctrine of prevenient grace viewed from a theological perspective. But how does it work "in us" from a more practical point of view? What happens to the person under the influence of prevenient grace? Wesley gave a twofold answer. First, prevenient grace works to *create awareness*. It awakens us to God and our need of salvation. Wesley believed we were awakened either by natural revelation or by the operation of the Law. God has left his footprints in creation. He is not contained in creation or equated with it, but he is revealed by it. Wesley believed that if any thoughtful person considered the beauty and complexity of the universe, he would have to consider the possibility of God's existence. There is too much around us that speaks of Someone greater than ourselves. And

---

[43]Jackson, *Works,* 6:511.

he also believed that if a person believed in the possibility of God, he would realize that if God exists, he matters completely. If God exists, the rest of life is defined in terms of him. If God exists, life is lived in relation to him. Through natural revelation these kinds of thoughts come to mind.

Wesley also believed that prevenient grace operated through the Law. He said, "It is the ordinary method of the Spirit of God to convict sinners by the Law."[44] The Law brings knowledge of God's will. With that knowledge we are able to see which side of the fence we are on. Through the Law we are able to see that we have fallen short of the glory of God. And out of this knowledge can flow a sense of need. We see ourselves as we really are. Our consciences are stirred.[45]

But Wesley knew that knowledge alone is not enough. Bare knowledge does not contain the power to change. In fact, knowledge without power leads to despair. We have all felt the frustration of knowing more than we were living up to. So Wesley knew that the will had to be brought into the picture. We change by action of the will. Therefore, prevenient grace operates in the second major way to *give us "response-ability."*

Here is an important point in Wesleyan theology. We have been told in Christianity that we are responsible for the sins we commit. Wesley saw that this could not be so if God had irrevocably decreed our destiny before the foundation of the world. Absolute decree undercuts authentic responsibility. Wesley taught that we can be held accountable only if we have genuine power of choice. He believed that prevenient grace enabled us to exercise our wills. *Through grace* we can be truly responsible!

---

[44]Jackson, *Works,* 5:443 (sermon: "The Original Nature, Property, and Use of the Law").

[45]Jackson, *Works,* 7:187 (sermon: "On Conscience").

There is risk here. If God has given us the power to choose through prevenient grace, he runs the risk of our choosing against him. But Wesley believed that wherever love was in operation, risk was always present. Love must be freely given and freely received. We have no problem in seeing God's free gift of love in Jesus Christ. Wesley wants us to see that our *response* to that gift is also free. In that kind of freedom there can be authentic relationship.

God has taken the risk. By his grace he has enabled us to respond. Everyone is included in the *offer* of salvation. No one is inescapably trapped in sin. No one is destined to hell because of the action of God. On the contrary, God is at work to win as many as possible to himself. Even in the darkest night of the soul there can be the dawning of light. It is light that points toward a door—a Way. It speaks to us in the sickness and paralyzing grip of sin and says, "Get up! Pick up your mat and walk."

If you have read this chapter as a Christian, you will be able to look into your past and see many of the ways God's prevenient grace operated in your life to bring you to the place of commitment. If you are reading this chapter as a non-Christian, you, too, will be able to reflect on those experiences that have shed light on your path. All of these experiences are examples of prevenient grace. The challenge is to act in accordance with what you have received and to respond to God if you will.

The message of prevenient grace is a message of hope. There *is* a way out of the human dilemma. There *is* a way out of our problems. God has made the way! And by his prevenient grace he enables us to walk in this way if we choose to do so. Prevenient grace is not the whole story, but it is the beginning. It is not the bright light of day, but it is the first light of dawn. It is real light—light enough to see the hand of God and to reach for it.

Questions for Reflection and Discussion

1. As you think of your life experiences, what events in your past before conversion would you consider activities of God's prevenient grace?

2. Do you agree that knowledge alone (without the power to change) is not sufficient? Are there any experiences in your life where this has been so?

3. How do you react to the statement that God holds us personally responsible only if we are *able* to respond? How does prevenient grace operate to make us truly responsible?

For Further Reading

Sermon: "Justification by Faith," in Jackson's *The Works of John Wesley,* 5:53–64.

Sermon: "The Witness of Our Own Spirit," in Jackson's *The Works of John Wesley,* 5:134–43.

Sermon: "On Conscience," in Jackson's *The Works of John Wesley,* 7:186–94.

Sermon: "On Working Out Our Own Salvation," in Jackson's *The Works of John Wesley,* 6:506–13.

Chapter Four

THE TURNING POINT
(CONVERTING GRACE)

---

*It is by the grace of God
that man turns, but he turns!*

FREDERICK NORWOOD

Light has broken through into the darkness! God has entered the human scene, made us aware of our condition, and offered us a way out. This is the first step in Wesley's understanding of the gospel. But he didn't stop here. He knew that prevenient grace was only the first light of dawn in the soul. It was a guide, which, if accepted, would lead a person to the brink of saving grace. Whenever Wesley spoke of prevenient grace, he encouraged his hearers to "stir up the spark of grace which is now in you, and God will give you more grace."[46] In this chapter we'll consider the next step in the activity of grace—exploring what Wesley called *saving grace.*

Whenever we speak of salvation, we are describing an experience that has two sides—a divine side and a human side. From the divine side, salvation is by grace *alone.* As Wesley put it, "There is nothing we are, or have, or do, which can deserve the least thing at God's hand."[47] The apostle Paul expressed it this way: "For it is by grace you have been saved" (Ephesians 2:8). It is only by divine action that anyone is saved. But God has acted! Through Christ justice has been done and grace has been given. Mercy has triumphed over condemnation. We have been saved *by grace!*

From the human side, salvation is by faith. Paul goes on to say, "For it is by grace you have been saved, through faith." Faith is the human response to divine grace. It is our reaction to God's

---

[46]Jackson, *Works,* 6:513 (sermon: "On Working Out Our Own Salvation").
[47]Jackson, *Works,* 5:7 (sermon: "Salvation by Faith").

prior action. But even faith is not of ourselves. It, too, is the gift of God, which he gives to us through prevenient grace. Prevenient grace enables us to make a faith response. So while faith issues from us, it does not originate in us.

For Wesley, the faith response was characterized by two movements—repentance and belief. Taken together, these constitute "saving faith." Wesley is clearly one with the biblical revelation. Both John the Baptist and Jesus began their public ministries with the call to repent (see Matthew 3:2; 4:17). When Paul defended his ministry before King Agrippa, he declared that his message was that people "should repent and turn to God" (Acts 26:20). When Wesley proclaimed the message of saving grace, he focused on the same terms: *repent* and *believe*.

But what does it mean to repent? Sadly, some people associate it with negative images. Others identify it with going to an altar. Still others view it primarily in terms of sorrow. However, when the New Testament speaks of repentance, it uses the basic idea of *change*. Wesley called it "a change of heart from all sin to all holiness."[48] He meant that, whereas we once lived in sin with little thought of God, now we have had a change of mind. Now we know that sin matters; it must be forsaken. Now we know that God matters; he must be followed. We have made a 180-degree turn. Tears may or may not be involved. An altar may be the place of repentance, but so may our living room at home. In either state or location the principle remains; we have changed. And Wesley believed this change would affect us in several ways.

First, we change in the *knowledge* of ourselves. We now see ourselves as living apart from God. Wesley urged his followers, "Know thyself to be a sinner. Know that corruption of thy inmost nature. Know that thou art corrupted in every power."[49] In repen-

---

[48]Wesley, *Explanatory Notes Upon the New Testament* (note on Matthew 3:8).
[49]Jackson, *Works,* 5:82 (sermon: "The Way to the Kingdom").

tance we have a change of heart about our spiritual condition. Apart from God we are not "okay." We are in a desperate condition. Wesley calls us to see ourselves realistically. This is the first effect of repentance.

Second, we experience further change through *conviction*. When we realize the true condition of our lives apart from God, we are pricked in our hearts. Wesley believed that in conviction God impressed on our minds the fact of our guilt and our deserving of eternal destruction.[50] Such a self-understanding would weigh heavy on us. But while the picture is unpleasant, Wesley never intended it to be negative. Rather, conviction was viewed as a part of God's *positive* action in our lives.

Unfortunately, we have often pictured conviction in negative images. We have used it to create guilt feelings in our hearers. To some it means primarily that we have finally been caught. When conviction is expressed in these ways, it is viewed as something to get away from, something to be thrown off—like getting out from under a spiritual hornets' nest. On the contrary, the truer picture is that conviction indicates our hearts are still sensitive enough for God's Spirit to touch them. It is proof positive that our souls are still open enough for the risen Christ to enter. Conviction is a positive experience, although it may be unpleasant. It is the "warning light of the soul" that lets us know that all is *not* well. Adjustments need to be made.

In non-Christians conviction works to bring them to the place of salvation. As a surgeon's knife must cut before it can cure, so conviction must come before we can find victory over sin. But conviction is not limited to those outside the faith. Christians continue to be convicted as the Holy Spirit prompts us to make midcourse corrections. In this dimension Wesley recognized the need for repentance in believers.

---

[50]Jackson, *Works*, 5:81.

Third, repentance includes a thorough *change of our minds*.[51] This is the true end of repentance. It is illustrated most perfectly in the story of the prodigal son in Luke 15. After the younger son left home, his condition deteriorated rapidly. He ended up in the pigpen. While there he came to a new self-understanding. He saw the contrast between life there and life at home. Self-knowledge led to the conviction that he had sinned and that he should return home. So far, so good. But if he had stopped there, he would have stayed in the pigpen forever. Another step was needed. He had to *engage his will*. He needed to *act on his conviction*. The process of repentance was completed when he said, "I will set out and go back to my father."

Repentance climaxes in the determination to go home. The step has to be taken, or else all the self-knowledge and conviction in the world will not suffice. Wesley is scriptural and realistic in calling for action in repentance. We need to be changed—and repentance calls for change.

Before leaving the matter of repentance, it is important to note that Wesley believed repentance comes before true belief. In a sermon he made this observation:

> We must repent before we can believe the gospel. We must be cut off from dependency upon ourselves before we can truly depend on Christ. We must cast away all confidence in our own righteousness, or we cannot have a true confidence in His. Till we are delivered from trusting in anything that we do, we cannot thoroughly trust in what He has done and suffered. First, we receive the sentence of death in ourselves: then we trust in Him that lived and died for us.[52]

---

[51]Jackson, *Works,* 5:83.
[52]Jackson, *Works,* 5:241 (sermon: "The Lord Our Righteousness").

But even repentance is not the end of the process. Wesley called repentance "the porch of religion."[53] The second major part of saving grace is *faith*. Wesley knew it wasn't sufficient just to get away from the problem. We must move toward the solution. It is not sufficient to turn *from* something; we must turn *toward* Someone.

Jesus taught this clearly in Matthew 12:43–45. He told of the person who had an evil spirit. The person "cleaned house" and was rid of the demon. The old was gone. The life was cleaned up and aired out. But it was empty. One day the evil spirit strolled by and noticed the house. It was in better shape than ever! The demon had an idea. He went and called seven of his friends, and they all entered into the person's life. Jesus said the end result was worse than the first. Why? Because he had only gone halfway. The old was gone, but he had not embraced the new. In his emptiness, he was vulnerable.

The same is true in the process of saving grace. Repentance is not enough. It is like one act of a two-act drama. Act two is necessary to complete the play. Act two is *belief*.

Because *belief* is a common term in Christianity, it is necessary to see what Wesley meant by it. It is clear what he did not mean. He did not mean mere intellectual assent to a creed or a statement of faith. He did not mean only the rational activity of the mind:

> Only beware thou dost not deceive thy own soul, with regard to the nature of this faith. It is not, as some have fondly conceived, a bare assent to the truth of the Bible, or the articles of our creed, or of all that is contained in the Old and New Testaments. The devils believe this . . . and yet they are devils still.[54]

---

[53]Telford, *Letters*, 2:268.
[54]Jackson, *Works*, 5:85.

The preceding remarks should not be taken to mean that Wesley minimized the intellectual dimension of faith. His own life disproves that. He sought whenever possible to have a reasonable faith. But it does mean that he knew that belief, in the scriptural sense, involved much more. He included at least four strands in his understanding of it.

First, belief means to put your confidence, your trust, in the mercy and forgiveness of God. Wesley put it this way: "To believe in God implies, to trust in him as our strength, without whom we can do nothing . . . as our help, our only help in time of trouble."[55] Through prevenient grace we see the greatness of our sin, but we know our salvation is greater. We know we deserve punishment but we believe we shall receive mercy! We have a sure confidence in the mercy and forgiveness of God.

Return to the story of the prodigal son. It was repentance that awakened him to his condition, brought him to conviction, and motivated him to change. But it was faith that gave him the confidence to know that when he returned home, he would be loved and forgiven. He knew mercy would triumph over judgment. If he had not believed that, he would never have dared to go home.

Repentance and faith go hand in hand. Repentance breeds awareness; belief fosters confidence. And our belief is rooted in the nature of God. We believe God is *love*. So we also believe he is more willing to heal us than hurt us, to receive us than to turn us away. In the words of 1 John 4:18, "Perfect love drives out fear." We are not afraid to go home!

Wesley preached the love of God because he was convinced that when anyone was gripped by this love, he would want to go home. Sadly, there are still many who do not have this concept of God. Having a basically negative concept, they are not

---

[55]Jackson, *Works,* 5:380 (Sermon XXIX: "Upon Our Lord's Sermon on the Mount," Discourse IX).

moved to establish a relationship with him. But if we can accept a God who is *love*—love by nature and love by choice—yes, we can love a God like that!

The second element in belief is *assurance*. More will be said about this in the next chapter, but it's important to see the relationship between saving faith and assurance. Saving faith brings a note of certainty into our lives. Through faith we know that Jesus is truly the Son of God. We see Jesus as the only foundation of salvation.[56] It is interesting to note how the theme of assurance runs through Wesley's record of his experience at Aldersgate:

> I felt my heart strangely warmed. I felt I did trust in Christ, Christ alone for salvation: And an assurance was given me that he had taken away my sin, even mine, and saved me from the law of sin and death.[57]

Wesley saw *reliance* as the third element in belief. In the act of faith we switch the control center of our lives from ourselves to Christ. In the past we relied on our own power and intellect, but now we rely on Christ. The early church described this reliance in the affirmation "Jesus is Lord." By this they meant initially a reliance on Christ to save them from their sins. Wesley likewise saw the cross as the focal point of our deliverance. He wrote, "Nothing in the Christian system is of greater consequence than the doctrine of the Atonement."[58]

But to affirm Christ's lordship also means that we look to him for life in the present. We serve a risen Savior. We acknowledge him to be our sovereign, provider, and empowerer. Here is where the dynamic of Wesleyan discipleship is seen. Through saving faith we appropriate the power of Christ to and for every

---

[56]Jackson, *Works*, 5:137 (sermon: "The Witness of Our Own Spirit").
[57]Jackson, *Works*, 1:103 (Journal, 24 May 1738).
[58]Telford, *Letters*, 6:297–98.

dimension of our lives. He forgives the past, heals the present, and offers hope for the future. Consequently, reliance never ceases. In this way we can affirm with the saints of the ages, "I have been saved, I am being saved, and I shall be saved."

For Wesley, belief was ultimately expressed in *obedience*. The test of "knowing Christ" is whether or not we obey him. We do not go far in our Christian walk before we discover the troublesomeness of this truth. We quickly learn that it is one thing to profess faith, but it is something else to express it. Wesley drove this point home whenever he could. And he understood obedience in the broadest of terms. He described it as "obedience to all the commands of God, internal and external; obedience of the heart and of the life: in every temper and all manner of life."[59] Such obedience was not based on a cold sense of duty, but rather on an intense hunger to do God's will. Obedience is joyful, not legalistic. This doesn't mean that every experience will be easy, comfortable, or enjoyable. Some things are done "against the grain" and only by sheer force of the will. But it does mean that obedience to Christ—whether easy or difficult—will bring a sense of fulfillment to our lives.

This is the Wesleyan description of saving faith. It begins in repentance and climaxes in belief. In repentance we turn from a life without Christ; in belief we complete the turn by moving to embrace Christ's way as our way. And in that process, salvation is begun. Beyond the initial commitment there will be a lifetime of development and progress.

I hope this view of faith is inviting to you. It is a view that makes Christianity dynamic and not static. Too often we give the impression that our salvation is *completed* in a single dramatic experience. We hear endless testimonies of people who were saved "x" years ago. While Wesley would rejoice in this, he

---

[59]Jackson, *Works*, 5:220 (sermon: "The Marks of the New Birth").

would go on to ask, "But are you saved today, in this moment?" He would want to know if the experience of the past was still alive in the present.

Wesley had an interesting picture of salvation. He compared it to a house. He called repentance the porch of religion. Justification was the door. All the rooms in the house were facets of our sanctification. By using this analogy he was trying to tell us that after the experience of conversion, there is a whole house—lifetime— to be explored.[60] There are effects of salvation, continuing dimensions and implications of our conversion. We must continue to walk and grow. Otherwise we will remain only in the hallways of the total experience God has for us.

We are now standing at the door. In the chapters that follow, we must walk into and through some of the rooms. But perhaps here is a good place to stand for a moment, giving thanks to God for saving faith and committing ourselves to the lifelong quest of exploring all the rooms of our spiritual house.

Questions for Reflection and Discussion

1. The author describes salvation from two sides—divine and human. Is this a new way to look at it for you? If so, how do you respond to this perspective?
2. Which element in repentance strikes you as being most important? Why?
3. Which element in belief strikes you as being most important? Why?
4. How does your testimony reflect the truth that salvation is dynamic (ongoing), not static (completed in a single, past action)?

---

[60]Jackson, *Works*, 8:472. Cf. Telford, *Letters*, 2:268.

For Further Reading

Sermon: "Salvation by Faith," in Jackson's *The Works of John Wesley*, 5:7–16.

Sermon: "Scriptural Christianity," in Jackson's *The Works of John Wesley*, 5:37–52.

Sermon: "Justification by Faith," in Jackson's *The Works of John Wesley*, 5:53–64.

Sermon: "The Righteousness of Faith," in Jackson's *The Works of John Wesley*, 5:65–75.

Sermon: "The Way to the Kingdom," in Jackson's *The Works of John Wesley*, 5:76–86.

Sermon: "The Marks of the New Birth," in Jackson's *The Works of John Wesley*, 5:212–22.

Sermon: "Upon Our Lord's Sermon on the Mount," Discourse IX, in Jackson's *The Works of John Wesley*, 5:378–92.

Chapter Five

TRANSFORMATION
(EFFECTS OF SALVATION)

*In his conception of salvation Wesley combines
a sense of complete dependence on God with
a sense of man's complete responsibility.*

ROBERT W. BURTNER AND ROBERT E. CHILES

I still remember the first time I visited an electric power plant. Even though I was only a child, no one had to tell me I was in the presence of power. Just being there was enough to know it. Conversion is like that. Even though it has never happened to you before, you know you're in the presence of power. It is not a vague, imperceptible experience. It is an experience of power.

Christians believe there are some discernable effects of conversion. In this chapter we'll examine some of them. It is important to remember that we are not looking at separate experiences. What we will examine is all part of *one* experience. Wesley taught that there are several effects in the one experience of conversion. Keeping the picture of a rope in mind may help. A rope is a single thing, but it is made up of many strands. Likewise, in conversion, several things happen to us.

First of all, Wesley taught that we are *justified*. In teaching this he was one with the Protestant Reformers and the saints of the ages. He recognized that justification by faith was the heart of the gospel. By justification he meant what God does *for* us. Wesley saw that sin had rendered people incapable of saving themselves. The only option left was the intervention of God. When God intervened to justify us, he *pardoned us* for the sins of the past. Wesley wrote, "The plain scriptural notion of justification is pardon, the forgiveness of sins."[61]

Wesley ministered before the age of modern psychology, but he knew the liberating power of forgiveness. And he saw the

---

[61]Jackson, *Works*, 5:57 (sermon: "Justification by Faith").

totality of forgiveness. He spoke of the pardoned sinner and said, "His sins, all his past sins, in thought, word, and deed, are covered, are blotted out, shall not be remembered or mentioned against him, any more than if they had not been."[62] It is not surprising that people responded to Wesley's message, for he was addressing the problem of unresolved guilt. Many of his hearers felt the guilt but didn't know how to resolve it. Wesley made it clear that in Christ forgiveness is already a reality.

In my ministry I have run up against a practical problem in this regard. I have counseled those who said, "I guess I'm not forgiven because I can't forget it." Somewhere along the line they've gotten the idea that God's forgiveness and their ability to forget go hand in hand. But notice, God speaks through his Word and says, "*I*, even *I*, am he who . . . remembers your sins no more" (Isaiah 43:25, emphasis added). He does not say, "*You* will remember your sins no more." Only God can forgive *and* forget. Some of the things we've done will be in our memories as long as we live. The message of the gospel is not the erasure of memory but rather the healing of our memories. Through justification we have memory without condemnation. We are forgiven!

At the same time, we experience a second effect—*new birth*. This is what God does *in* us. Wesley called it God's activity of "renewing our fallen nature."[63] He used the analogy of physical birth to describe the process. In physical birth something comes into existence that has never been alive before. In conversion our spiritual nature comes alive in a way it has never been before.

For one thing, there is a renewal of the image of God. In the chapter dealing with original sin we saw that the Fall corrupted the image of God by radically weakening the natural

---

[62]Jackson, *Works*, 5:57.
[63]Jackson, *Works*, 6:71 (sermon: "The New Birth").

image and destroying the moral image. But Wesley saw new birth as the renewal of righteousness and true holiness—the renewal of the moral image. He called it "that great change which God works in the soul when he brings it into life; when he raises it from the death of sin to the life of righteousness."[64] By this act we are made new creatures in Christ and restored to the full humanity God intended for us before the Fall.

In physical birth there is passage from fetal to full existence. Such a passage is essential if there is to be mature life. We are meant to live outside the womb. In the new birth there is also passage. We pass from spiritual death to spiritual life. We are made to live beyond the confines of sin. Related to this is the idea of power. When we are born, we are empowered to accomplish certain things. Likewise, new birth empowers us to live above sin. These notions of the Christian's relationship to sin are some of the strongest points in Wesley's theology. He firmly believed that a Christian was enabled to overcome sin.

Unfortunately, Wesley has been misunderstood at this point. Some have interpreted him to mean the actual *eradication* of sin. By this they have given the impression that Wesley believed the possibility of sin is removed. It is best to let Wesley speak for himself. In the sermon "The Scripture Way of Salvation," here is what he said:

> Hence may appear the extreme mischievousness of that seemingly innocent opinion that there is no sin in a believer, that all sin is destroyed, root and branch, the moment a man is justified. By totally preventing that repentance which follows justification, it quite blocks up the way to sanctification. There is no place for repentance in him who believes there is no sin either in his heart or life. Consequently, there

---

[64]Jackson, *Works,* 6:71.

is no place for his being perfected in love, to which that repentance is indispensably necessary.[65]

Wesley makes it clear that sin remains in the one who is justified, but it does not have to reign.[66] The error in the idea of eradication is that it treats sin as a "thing." We've already seen that for Wesley, sin is relational, not substantial. Since it is not a thing, it cannot be excised like a surgeon removes a tumor. A better word than removal is *reconciliation,* which is a relational word. Reconciliation speaks of a process of restoring a relationship that has been estranged. For Wesley, that is what new birth does. It rebuilds the bridge between God and man. It reopens the lines of communication. It reactivates the relationship that sin has deadened. And when it is restored, there is no reason that it ever has to be destroyed again.

In saying that Wesley taught victory over sin, it is necessary to understand what he meant by *sin.* He tells us himself: "By sin, I have understood outward sin . . . an actual, voluntary transgression of the law, acknowledged to be such at the time it is transgressed."[67] It is *very* important to remember this. Wesley always left open the possibility of involuntary sin, but he did not believe this sin would bring God's condemnation.

On the other side of the coin, he believed that a person was so empowered at justification that he could, in every case, choose the way of righteousness. No Christian *has* to sin; no Christian is *inevitably* bound to sin. Wesley had examples of individuals who sinned after they were "born of God."[68] His conclusion was

---

[65]Jackson, *Works,* 6:51 (sermon: "The Scripture Way of Salvation"). The words "which follow justification" are added to interpret which repentance Wesley had in mind.

[66]Jackson, *Works,* 6:50.

[67]Jackson, *Works,* 5:227 (sermon: "The Great Privilege of Those That Are Born of God").

[68]Jackson, *Works,* 5:227–32.

that if a person did not continue to keep watch over his life, he could lapse into sin after justification. But he also wanted to stress that sinning after conversion is not a necessity.

With this in mind it is possible to see more clearly what Wesley meant by overcoming sin, namely, that in conversion God gives grace powerful enough to forgive us of all our *past* sins and to fortify our wills against any future situation that might lead us to sin. Wesley could conceive of no moment or event more powerful than the grace of God. Grace is always greater than sin. Any return to sin is a problem of the will, not a problem of grace. The new birth renews the image of God, and this renewal powerfully keeps us and moves us toward full maturity in Christ.

Consequently, Wesley could speak of the third strand—*initial sanctification.* Justification is what God does *for* us. New birth is what God does *in* us. Initial sanctification is what God *begins* in us. Wesley said that in conversion, inward and outward holiness begins.[69] And in this beginning a couple of important things happen that enable us to mature in the Christian life.

Real righteousness begins. For Wesley it was unthinkable that God would call persons something they were not.[70] In conversion God not only declares us righteous, he actually makes us righteous with the righteousness of Christ. It is not a perfected righteousness that needs no further development, but it is genuine righteousness.

This is consistent with our view of sin as disease. When medicine is given to us, we are made healthy with the healing power it brings. The doctor doesn't simply declare us to be well; he gives us something that works a real change in our bodies. We are made healthy with the health-giving properties of the

[69]Jackson, *Works,* 6:71–72.
[70]Jackson, *Works,* 10:203, 271–83.

medicine. The result is genuine healing. In the spiritual life this means that when God says, "You are righteous," he does not do it with no basis in fact or with his fingers crossed. Rather, we are infused with the righteousness of Christ, which genuinely transforms our character.

Related to this is an *authentic purity that begins*. In conversion our hearts are cleansed from sin and made fit dwelling places for the Spirit. The activity of the Spirit from within works to transform our total life. Personal holiness expands into social holiness. Salvation from sin becomes salvation for service. What God has done in our spirits, he now moves out to do in our bodies, minds, emotions, and relationships.

It is important to see that Wesley is speaking about *initial* sanctification. He never intended that we should rest in or rely on a single spiritual experience. By terming it *initial sanctification,* he was striving to keep the dynamism of grace and point to the need for future growth in grace, knowledge, and righteousness. It is not inappropriate to say that Wesley's theology can always be summarized in the exhortation to "Go on!"

Lane Adams wrote a book titled *How Come It's Taking Me So Long to Get Better?*[71] The title alone is intriguing, but he uses an illustration that comes close to capturing what Wesley meant. Adams writes that during World War II the American forces used a "beachhead strategy" to capture islands in the South Pacific. Their goal was to capture a piece of the island, no matter how small. Then from the beachhead they worked their way out until they could claim the entire island.

Wesley is saying something similar. At the moment of conversion, the Holy Spirit captures a portion of our lives for God. The extent of that initial capture varies with each person, and

---

[71]Lane Adams, *How Come It's Taking Me So Long to Get Better?* (Wheaton, Ill.: Tyndale House, 1975).

no one would claim (in looking back) that God got it all the first time. But he did get a place to call his own. And from that dimension of our lives, the Spirit began to move out until more and more of our lives came under his control. This is the Wesleyan dynamic of grace that recognizes genuine change and at the same time acknowledges the need for continued growth.

These then are the major effects of salvation. Justification gives us a new standing before God. New birth gives us a new power to deal with sin and live for Christ. And initial sanctification begins the authentic development of Christlike character and provides a base for the Holy Spirit to purify and empower our lives.

In this regard I find it helpful to keep the idea of a football game in mind. Every week millions of fans pack stadiums to watch their favorite teams compete. But what do you suppose would happen if people took their seats and then heard something like this over the loudspeaker: "Today we are arbitrarily beginning the game in the middle of the second quarter and supposing that the score is 21–14 in favor of the home team." People would look at each other in dismay. They would be confused and bewildered. They know you don't play football that way. They would ask, "What happened to the kickoff? There has to be a kickoff."

Jesus told Nicodemus that everyone *must* be born again (see John 3:3). You cannot leave it out. You cannot move on to other things. But at the same time you do not have the kickoff and then go home. There are four full quarters to play before the game is complete. The kickoff begins it all and sets the stage for the rest. Conversion begins it all. It brings to our lives those dynamics that enable us to live the rest of our lives for Christ. These effects are meant to lead us into the future and equip us for effective discipleship. Through conversion the Spirit of God is in us, not only to deal with the past, but also to give us a vision for the future. And as far as living is concerned, *that* is the best effect of salvation!

Questions for Reflection and Discussion

1. In what ways does Wesley's theology help you avoid the problem of looking back to a single conversion experience as the sum total of Christian experience?
2. How do you respond to Wesley's belief that God never calls persons something they are not?
3. Consider each term—*justification, new birth,* and *initial sanctification.* What importance does each have in your Christian experience?

For Further Reading

Sermon: "Salvation by Faith," in Jackson's *The Works of John Wesley,* 5:7–16.

Sermon: "The Scripture Way of Salvation," in Jackson's *The Works of John Wesley,* 6:43–54.

Sermon: "Justification by Faith," in Jackson's *The Works of John Wesley,* 5:53–64.

Sermon: "The First Fruits of the Spirit," in Jackson's *The Works of John Wesley,* 5:87–97.

Sermon: "The New Birth," in Jackson's *The Works of John Wesley,* 6:65–76.

Sermon: "The Marks of the New Birth," in Jackson's *The Works of John Wesley,* 5:212–22.

Sermon: "The Great Privilege of Those That Are Born of God," in Jackson's *The Works of John Wesley,* 5:223–33.

Sermon: "The Wilderness State," in Jackson's *The Works of John Wesley*, 6:77–90.

Sermon: "On Sin in Believers," in Jackson's *The Works of John Wesley*, 6:144–55.

Chapter Six

DON'T STOP NOW
(GROWTH IN GRACE)

What one believes about human nature and God's grace will have a direct bearing on the kind of Christian life one experiences.

MILDRED WYNKOOP

Wesley's theology is a theology of grace. No matter where we are in our spiritual life, we got there by grace and we can go on in grace. The call of the Christian is the call to grow. The Wesleyan equation is this: "Grace plus response equals growth." There is no point in life where we can say, "I have all I need."

But how do we grow? Wesley believed that God has provided certain experiences and means by which we may grow in grace. One of the major emphases in Wesley's ministry was to nurture people in their faith. Unfortunately, this dimension of his ministry has often been overshadowed by his role as a traveling evangelist. While it is true that Wesley traveled far and wide to win people to Christ, it is equally true that, having won them, he sought to make disciples of them. He wanted more than bare converts or spiritual infants. He wanted people who were able to live the Christian life day by day and who could in turn bring others to faith. Therefore, he emphasized elements that contribute to growth in grace.

First, he taught that we grow in grace out of a sense of *assurance*. An assured faith is one of the central themes in Wesleyan theology. Wesley's favorite text in this regard was Romans 8:16: "The Spirit himself testifies with our spirit that we are God's children." In the early days of his ministry he felt so strongly about assurance that he taught there was no authentic salvation without it. By the mid-1740s he had modified his position, saying that, while assurance was not *necessary* for salvation, it was the "common privilege of all believers."[72]

Here, as at other times, Wesley let experience be his teacher. In his ministry he had found those persons who could testify to a salvation experience but who were still plagued by doubts and questions. He came to see this as one of the tools of Satan to rob the new believer of joy, peace, and power. Consequently, he preached the doctrine of assurance all the more, but now for motivation to grow rather than as a condition for salvation.

We can understand this if we return to Wesley's understanding of Christianity as a relationship. Authentic growth takes place when there is security and love in a relationship. Wesley said this is exactly what the Holy Spirit provides. He comes to our hearts to let us know that we are God's children. We do not have to live with a "hope so, think so, maybe so" faith. United Methodist pastor Ed Robb has said that if salvation is so insignificant that you can have it and not know it, then you can lose it and not tell it. It is the ministry of the Holy Spirit to bear witness to us that we *are* the children of God.

Unfortunately, assurance has been misunderstood. Some see it as impossible. They maintain it is not part of what God chooses to give his children. The best we can do is live with a rather high degree of tentativeness. For such people, to speak of assurance undercuts any motivation to growth. But we have shown (and will demonstrate further) that Wesley himself preached assurance as a motivation to growth. Assurance was not Methodism's "eternal security." For Wesley, assurance dealt with one's *present* relationship; it was no guarantee for the future. Only continued obedience and faithfulness could take care of the future.

---

[72]Telford, *Letters,* 2:91. Robert Tuttle's book *John Wesley: His Life and Theology* has a helpful discussion of Wesley's views on assurance on pages 199–211.

Still others have seen any testimony of assurance as an expression of pride. They say, "To speak of an assured faith sounds like spiritual conceit." To be sure, if one testifies to assurance based on any special experience or performance, it is conceit. For Wesley, true assurance is *not* saying, "Look what a great Christian I am!" Rather it is saying, "Look what a great Savior I have!" Here is the point of assurance: Christ has powerfully entered our lives, and it is his intention to stay.

Despite misunderstandings, legitimate questions remain: Is there anything on which to base assurance? Can we distinguish between true assurance and presumption? Is there a way to be sure we are not fooling ourselves? Wesley would answer yes to these questions. He provided a series of tests which a person could use to judge the authenticity of his assurance.[73]

First, he taught, as Paul declared, that there is the witness of the Spirit. The Holy Spirit will not call us something we are not. Wesley wrote, "We must be holy of heart and holy in life before we can be conscious that we are so."[74] The first movement is God's. We love him because he *first* loved us (see 1 John 4:19). Wesley wanted it to be clearly understood that assurance has an objective base. We do not dream it up. It is a gift from God, mediated to us through the Holy Spirit and on the basis of Christ's atonement.[75] When the Spirit bears witness, he does so to something that has actually occurred.

Second, there is the test of the witness of our own spirit. When we examine ourselves, we can be aware of at least four elements that confirm God's grace in our lives:

---

[73]Jackson, *Works,* 5:117–23 (sermon: "The Witness of the Spirit").
[74]Jackson, *Works,* 5:115.
[75]Jackson, *Works,* 5:115.

1. We know that we have repented of our sins. In the last chapter we showed that repentance does not happen apart from the exercise of our wills. It is a conscious determination to change. Therefore, Wesley said, we can know that we have repented.
2. We are aware of a change in our lives. Wesley called it a change from darkness to light, from the power of Satan to the power of God.[76]
3. We are aware of a new character produced in us. Here is where the fruit of the Spirit comes in (see Galatians 5:22–23).
4. We find joy in the service of God. Wesley said, "A true lover of God hastens to do His will on earth as it is done in heaven."[77]

Through these tests, Wesley believed that any person could distinguish between true assurance and presumption. Having come to the conclusion that assurance is well-founded, he believed we would be joyously motivated to grow in the grace and knowledge of Jesus Christ.

Wesley's second major teaching on growth in grace had to do with the practical ways in which such growth takes place. For him, it occurred through the use of the means of grace. *The means of grace* was a particular term in Protestant and Roman Catholic circles to describe the specific channels through which God conveys grace to his people. Wesley never limited God's grace to these "means"; he only believed that the means of grace were the normal (ordinary) ways that God enabled the believer to grow in grace.[78]

---

[76]Jackson, *Works*, 5:118–19.
[77]Jackson, *Works*, 5:120.
[78]Jackson, *Works*, 5:187 (sermon: "The Means of Grace").

Before discussing the various means of grace, a general statement is in order. Wesley did not believe that the means of grace had any power in themselves. The use of them did not alone guarantee growth in grace. The means of grace were just that—means, not ends in themselves. Therefore, when he advocated the use of the means of grace, it was never in a legalistic or mechanistic sense. But he did believe that these usual channels were used by God to communicate his grace to people. He divided the means of grace into two groups—the instituted means (those ordained by Christ), and the prudential means (those ordained by the church). The instituted means were his primary focus, but he also taught that God has chosen to work through the prudential means as well.

The first instituted means of grace is *prayer*. It comes first in Wesley's list because of his understanding of Christianity as a relationship. He called prayer "the grand means of drawing near to God" and felt that all the other means should be mixed with prayer.[79] At the heart was Wesley's knowledge that all relationships—human and divine—require good communication. He recognized prayer as the means of this communication between God and man.

In one of my own revival meetings a man came confessing spiritual dryness. Inquiring about his relationship with God, I discovered he had not prayed with regularity or meaning for over a year. As we kept talking, I began to sense that this was the heart of his problem. The lines of communication were down; consequently he was not receiving any fresh word from God or feeling that his words were reaching their intended destination.

Wesley called the lack of prayer the common cause of "the wilderness state" (a sense of spiritual dryness and purposelessness).

---

[79]Telford, *Letters,* 4:90.

He went on to say that the lack of prayer in one's life cannot be made up for by any other means.[80] Because he believed in the indispensable nature of prayer, Wesley urged his people to be faithful in private and public prayer. His own life was a model of discipline and regularity in prayer. The hours of every day were undergirded and saturated with prayer. As a result, he experienced growth in grace.

The second instituted means of grace is what Wesley called *searching the Scriptures*. He knew the power of the Bible. He referred to himself as a man of one book, and he wanted Methodists to be Bible Christians.[81] To aid his followers in the use of Scripture, he compiled explanatory notes for both the Old and New Testaments and made them available at reasonable prices.[82] Wesley's emphasis on the primacy of Scripture was based on the conviction that through the Bible God gives, confirms, and increases true wisdom.

Accordingly, Wesley laid down certain principles that would increase one's knowledge of the Word and allow it to have its greatest effect. First, he wanted a person to know the whole Bible, not just parts of it. He advocated reading from both Testaments each day. Second, he did believe that a regular reading of the Bible was most profitable for spiritual growth. His own practice was usually to follow the suggested readings in the table of lessons in the Book of Common Prayer. However, he maintained an inner freedom to read wherever he felt God was directing him. Third, he believed that one should carefully apply and immediately put into practice what was read. He had little use for a detached reading of Scripture. Instead, he wanted

---

[80]Jackson, *Works*, 6:81 (sermon: "The Wilderness State").

[81]See Telford, *Letters*, 4:299; Jackson, *Works*, vol. 11; Jackson, *Works*, 8:339–47 for Wesley's view concerning his own life and the lives of early Methodists.

[82]*Explanatory Notes Upon the New Testament* was published in 1755, and *Explanatory Notes Upon the Old Testament* followed in 1765.

readers to ask, "What does this mean for me?" and "How can I put the truth of Scripture to work for the good of others?" In this way, the Bible served as an important means of grace.

The Lord's Supper stood third in the instituted means of grace. Wesley averaged communing once every four or five days. He exhorted early Methodists to practice "constant communion," which included being present whenever possible at Holy Communion. On many occasions he personally led Methodists from their preaching houses to the Anglican parish churches in order that they might receive the sacrament. When Anglicans no longer welcomed Methodists at their altars, he found other legitimate ways of providing the Lord's Supper for his followers.

Why was he so concerned that the Methodists receive the sacrament at every opportunity? Because he believed that the experience was more than a symbol; it was an opportunity to actually commune with Christ and receive the grace of God. He stopped short of any notion of transubstantiation, but he believed that Christ was present in the service. Normally, the Lord's Supper would be of greatest benefit to believers, an aid to growth in grace. But Wesley also believed that the sacrament had a converting potential. Consequently, his invitation was an open one, extended to anyone who truly and earnestly repented of sin, was in love and charity with neighbor, and intended to lead a new life following God's commandments. This being so, the Lord's Supper became the high point in early Methodist worship.[83]

The fourth instituted means of grace was *fasting*. In the earlier part of his life and ministry, Wesley observed Wednesdays and Fridays as fast days—in keeping with the practices of the

---

[83]One of the finest treatments of Wesley's view of the Lord's Supper is John Bowmer's *The Sacrament of the Lord's Supper in Early Methodism* (London: Dacre Press, 1951).

early Christians. Later on, he dropped Wednesday and exhorted his followers to faithfully keep Friday as a day of fasting. It is important to see that Wesley did not see fasting as an act of mortification, or as a lengthy experience. He did not believe the effectiveness of fasting lay in its duration or intensity but rather in the commitment of time exclusively for God and spiritual concerns.

Normally, Wesley began his fast after the evening meal on Thursday evening and broke it with tea on Friday afternoon. In between he gave particular time to prayer and devotion. When the occasion demanded, he was open to longer fasts. But as an ongoing means of grace he felt this regular practice was sufficient. Through these weekly fasts he believed God mediated grace to enrich the Christian life.[84]

The fifth instituted means of grace was *group fellowship,* or what Wesley called "Christian conference." As it turned out, this means became the primary instrument of early Methodist renewal. Wherever Wesley preached, he sought to organize believers into bands, classes, and societies for their continuing nurture. In 1743, he organized these groups into the *united societies,* a movement within the Church of England. Methodism remained as a "little church" within the larger body until shortly after Wesley's death.

It is interesting to see the various dynamics at work in these three units of Methodist nurture. The *bands* were groups of four to eight people of the same gender and as near the same maturity in Christ as possible. Wesley believed that every Christian needed a small, intimate place to share the concerns of his or her life and to find commonality of experience and intensity of support. The *classes* were groups of about a dozen, mixed as to gender and levels of experience. In time the classes became the

---

[84]Jackson, *Works,* 5:344–60 (Sermon XXVII: "Upon Our Lord's Sermon on the Mount," Discourse VII).

core of Methodist nurture, often being led by laypersons. The class leader functioned as an undershepherd and was responsible for the spiritual and temporal welfare of those in the group. The *societies* were the largest group in Methodism per se, usually numbering more than forty. Societies met weekly for Bible exposition, singing, testimony, and prayer. When clergymen were available, they gave leadership to the societies, but often these groups were led by the laity as well. On each level, the dynamic was different, but the total experience provided a nearly comprehensive experience of nurture and discipleship.

The importance Wesley placed in this means of grace can be seen in two remarks he made. On one occasion he stated that "preaching like an apostle without joining together those that are awakened and training them up in the ways of God, is only begetting children for the murderer."[85] This was his opinion after a visit to Pembrokeshire where there were no regular societies. His evaluation was that "the consequence is that nine of the ten once-awakened are now faster asleep than ever."[86] He was fully convinced that wherever this dimension of discipleship was lost, Methodism would cease to be a vital movement.

These are the five instituted means of grace. Wesley believed that God had ordained them as channels through which his converting and confirming grace could flow. In addition to these, Wesley recognized three prudential means of grace: doing no harm, doing all the good you can, and attending the private and public worship of God.[87] He used these means as conditions for continuing membership in the Methodist societies, and members were regularly examined to see how they were living up to such standards.

---

[85]Jackson, *Works*, 3:144.
[86]Jackson, *Works*, 3:144.
[87]Jackson, *Works*, 8:323–24.

At the heart of it was Wesley's conviction that growth in grace is not accidental or automatic. One does not wander or stumble into maturity. On God's side, he does not save us and then tell us to do the best we can. Rather, he supplies specific instruments through which he can nurture us. To be sure, he is not limited to these means, but he has chosen to use them as his primary and normal means of effecting Christian growth. I have yet to meet a vital, growing Christian who did not use these means of grace in one way or another.

There will always be highs and lows, ups and downs, advances and declines. Christians have good days and bad days, just like everyone else. Not to admit this is to misrepresent the facts. There are mountaintop experiences, but they don't come every day. The key to Christian growth is not feeling but *faithfulness*. God has expressed his faithfulness by providing means of grace. We express our faithfulness by taking advantage of them. And in that divine/human encounter, the connection is made, grace flows into our lives, and we are led to greater conformity to the image of Christ.

Questions for Reflection and Discussion

1. Consider the equation "Grace plus response equals growth." What does this mean for your life right now?
2. Did the treatment of Wesley's view of assurance shed any new light on the issue for you?
3. Review the various means of grace. Then (1) share a growth experience you have had in relation to one of them, and (2) share any needs you may be feeling regarding them.

4. Overall, would you say your faith is growing or standing still? How are the means of grace helping, or how could they help, as you chart your course for the future?

For Further Reading

Sermon: "The Witness of the Spirit" (Discourse Two), in Jackson's *The Works of John Wesley*, 5:123–33.

Sermon: "The Witness of Our Own Spirit," in Jackson's *The Works of John Wesley*, 5:134–43.

Sermon: "The Wilderness State," in Jackson's *The Works of John Wesley*, 6:77–90.

Sermon: "The Means of Grace," in Jackson's *The Works of John Wesley*, 5:185–201.

Sermon: "Upon Our Lord's Sermon on the Mount," Discourse VII, in Jackson's *The Works of John Wesley*, 5:344–60.

Sermon: "The Duty of Constant Communion," in Jackson's *The Works of John Wesley*, 7:147–57.

"The Nature, Design, and General Rules of the United Societies in London, Bristol, Kingswood, etc.," in Jackson's *The Works of John Wesley*, 8:269–71.

"Rules of the Band-Societies," in Jackson's *The Works of John Wesley*, 8:272–74.

Chapter Seven

THE HEART OF IT ALL
(CHRISTIAN PERFECTION)

*It is good to know that after the passage of
another century, Methodist theologians are once
more exploring the important truths underlined
in Wesley's teaching on Christian Perfection.*

FRANK BAKER

Wesley viewed the doctrine of Christian perfection as the "grand depositum" of Methodism. He believed that God had raised up the people called Methodist to proclaim this truth.[88] Sadly, there is no element in Wesley's theology that causes more trouble today than this one. On one extreme are those who virtually ignore the doctrine. On the other extreme are those who would make Christian perfection the all-important element in Christian experience and the window through which the rest of Wesleyan theology is viewed. In between are the vast majority of mainline Methodists who either have not heard the doctrine or who have been confused by what they have heard. Either case is unfortunate, for it leaves Wesley's doctrine in a position he never intended.

Before much progress can be made, two things need to be admitted. First, the doctrine of Christian perfection cannot be omitted from any serious examination of Wesley's theology. Nor can it be omitted from a contemporary interpretation of Christian experience. Second, Wesley does not answer every question we would like to ask about the doctrine. The result is a kind of tension between items one and two—a tension that can never be fully resolved. We are left to interpret the doctrine as faithfully as we can, knowing that we are in the spirit of Wesley when we do.

The place to begin is with the word *perfection*. This more than anything else throws people off the track—and that right

---

[88]Telford, *Letters*, 8:238. It is important to note that this was written less than a year before Wesley's death. He held this view throughout his lifetime.

at the start. They hear the word and exclaim, "No one can be *perfect!*" Obviously not, if you mean perfection in terms of absolute purity or flawless performance. But Wesley did not use the term *perfection* in that sense. We miss the point if we read a dictionary definition of the word and equate it with Wesley's definition. Notice that he modified *perfection* with the significant adjective *Christian*. Immediately, the term is put in a new context. Wesley is advocating *Christian* perfection, which puts it in a new and attainable light. We will see how this is so as we move along.

But even Christian perfection has its limits. For one thing, it is not spiritual infallibility. Wesley made it plain that the Christian is still liable to sin and does not possess absolute knowledge, absolute judgment, or absolute performance.[89] Wesley termed such notions "angelism" and felt that to make it appear so high was to effectually renounce it.[90] Wesley constantly maintained that Christian perfection is for real people in this life.

Second, Christian perfection does not make one a superior Christian. Wesley rejected any idea of a status system among believers. On the contrary, he felt that anyone who experienced Christian perfection would be filled with humility.[91] Such a one would never entertain the idea of being better than anyone else. As with everything else in the Christian faith, the experience of Christian perfection is of *grace*—not of works, lest anyone should boast.

Third, Christian perfection is not immunity from life's problems. In fact, Satan seems to delight in defeating those who are closest to God (see 1 Peter 5:8). Christians are exposed to the same germs, the same natural laws, and the same temptations

---

[89]Jackson, *Works,* 6:2–7 (sermon: "Christian Perfection").
[90]Telford, *Letters,* 5:20.
[91]Jackson, *Works,* 11:427.

as any other person.[92] Christian perfection is not a vaccination against reality.

Fourth, Christian perfection is not a static, onetime experience. To be sure, Wesley identified it with a spiritual *crisis* (significant event) in one's pilgrimage. He taught that a person could be entirely sanctified in an instant.[93] But it is important to note that he never separated the "moment" from one's total Christian experience. When Wesley spoke of the instantaneous nature of Christian perfection he usually stressed the process that precedes and follows it.[94] The event was always kept in balance with the larger activity of God's grace.

No illustration perfectly captures what is going on here, but I have come to see it as analogous to the relationship between a moment of time and time itself. Place a clock in front of you. Once a day on this clock it is precisely "high noon." For a *moment* it is exactly twelve o'clock. This moment is real and necessary. In fact, if you have a camera, you can take a picture the instant the second hand sweeps across the twelve. You can capture and describe that moment. But "high noon" loses its significance when it is divorced from the movement of the second hand before and after the moment itself. Moments in time are only meaningful in light of the fact that *time moves*.

Christian perfection is like that. There is sanctifying grace that may operate in one's life "in a moment." The experience can be noted and described. But the experience loses its full significance when it is divorced from the larger activity of grace before and after. God's grace leads us to the place of Christian perfection (narrowly viewed), and it leads us on after the experience itself. That's why Wesley could urge those

[92]Jackson, *Works*, 6:5.
[93]Jackson, *Works*, 11:446.
[94]Jackson, *Works*, 11:446.

who testified to this experience to "go on to perfection" in the ultimate, heavenly sense.

Having looked at some of the things Christian perfection is not, we may now move to a consideration of its positive features. It is important not to misunderstand the experience, but it is more important to explore the actual dynamics of it. Most important of all, it is *singleness of intention*. The heart of Christian perfection is in the will, not in one's actions. Actions vary, while intentions can remain constant.[95]

To speak of Christian perfection as singleness of intention does not minimize actions, but it does mean that the experience of *being* is deeper than the level of *doing*. It means we have discovered a central purpose for life—a purpose that gives meaning, direction, and power to life. For Wesley, the central purpose was captured in Matthew 22:37–39 ("Love the Lord your God with all your heart. . . . Love your neighbor as yourself"). Wesley saw (as did many before him) that the primary intention, the controlling desire, is our resolve to love God and others.

But how can this love be called *perfect* by God while at the same time be flawed? An illustration from parenting can provide a clue. When each of my children were small, they had the bright idea to bring Mommy some flowers. Never mind that they plucked the flowers from the bed Mommy had worked hard to cultivate. Never mind that they may have even taken flowers from the neighbor's bed! Their one desire was to please Mommy and to show their love for her. So in they came with flowers, weeds, and dirt. With faces aglow they exclaimed, "Mommy, we love you!"

---

[95]Wesley borrowed here from the rich tradition of the past, particularly from the Eastern church fathers (for example, Gregory of Nyssa) and from persons like Thomas à Kempis, Juliana of Norwich, Françis Fénelon, Jeremy Taylor, and William Law. All of these (and many others) placed the heart of Christianity in one's intentions and motives—often calling it "perfect love."

What did Mommy do? Did she throw the flowers away because they had clumps of weeds and grass clinging to them? Did she refuse to accept them because they were pulled from her bed or the bed of a neighbor? Of course not! She saw the deed through the eyes of love, took her nicest vase, and proudly displayed the flowers on the table. She accepted the act of love, even though she might follow it up (at an appropriate time) with a lesson in flower-picking.

So it is with God. He accepts our intentions. He sees our motives. It has to be this way, for in the light of his impeccable holiness even our best actions fall short. The Bible puts it this way: Even our best actions look like filthy rags in comparison to God (see Isaiah 64:6). We cannot hope to match him in actions, but we can be one with him in motive. Our controlling desire can be to do his will on earth as it is in heaven. God knows whether or not this is our intention, and when it is, he calls it perfect, even though it comes packaged with some weeds and dirt.

By taking this approach, God does not ignore or minimize sin. Even perfect Christians are convicted when their actions and attitudes are improper.[96] Like a good parent, God has to take us aside, point out our mistakes, and teach us how to bring our lives into greater conformity to his will. But the point is that he does not negate the relationship when performance is flawed. Those of us who are married know that we operate under this system every day. If we have to relate to each other in marriage— and in fact we *want* to relate to each other this way—*how much more* is God willing to do the same!

The beautiful irony is that by starting with intentions first, God more powerfully moves us to change than if he started with legalism. Counselors' offices are filled with people who experienced both discipline without love and legalism without affection. Such

[96]Jackson, *Works*, 5:156–70 (sermon: "The Repentance of Believers").

persons struggle with low self-esteem and buried resentment toward parents, friends, and associates who never loved them. But when we know we are loved, believed in, and trusted, we really want to do the best we can.

The implications here are numerous, but for the moment it is important to see the connection between motives and actions. Wesley wrote before the days of modern psychology, but he is amazingly contemporary here. He knew that our actions would be more consistent when our motives are fixed. Together with Jesus, he affirmed that it is out of the heart where deeds are expressed (see Matthew 12:35).

So we begin with the powerful truth that Christian perfection is singleness of intention. But secondly, it is *power over sin*.[97] Simply put, Wesley did not believe there was ever a time when a person *had* to sin. In any conceivable situation the grace of God is always greater than the lure of temptation. Wesley knew that as long as we are in the body, temptations to sin will always be there. But he believed that the love of God at work in the heart of a person could exclude actual transgression both inwardly and outwardly. The key was to "abide in Christ"—to dwell in the presence of this powerful God.[98]

Notice that intention is related to this dimension as well. If we have settled the issue of sin by a previous commitment to love God and neighbor, then when actual temptations present themselves, power will be there to overcome. Wesley was a realist in acknowledging that even sanctified Christians can sin.[99] But he attributed any departures as a failure of will, not a failure of grace. In Christian perfection there is power to overcome sin.

---

[97]Jackson, *Works*, 5:223–33 (sermon: "The Great Privilege of Those That Are Born of God").

[98]Jackson, *Works*, 5:232.

[99]Jackson, *Works*, 5:232.

Third, Wesley taught that Christian perfection is *radical dependence on Christ.*[100] Such dependence is total and continuous. It is the recognition that whatever we are and do is the result of Christ's power at work in us. In Wesley's covenant service this was epitomized in the vine-branch relationship of John 15. Here the idea of *connection* predominates. As long as we are connected to Christ, there will be life, growth, fruit, power, and joy. The perfecting grace of God binds us more closely to Christ.

Dr. J. T. Seamands has described this deepening dependency by speaking of Christian perfection as the movement of Christ in our lives from resident to president. E. Stanley Jones often spoke of it as our act of "full surrender." Robert Munger described it in his booklet *My Heart Christ's Home* as giving Christ every "room" (dimension) of your life, even the closet where yesterday's sin and guilt are stored. In all these ways Christian writers are impressing on us the fact that, as we allow Christ to be Lord over our lives, we increasingly sense our need of him.

Fourth, Christian perfection is *equipment for ministry.* One of the meanings of sanctification is that we are *set apart* for the service of God. Wesley recognized that Christian perfection is not only a personal experience but also a social imperative. He called those who testified to the experience of Christian perfection to "do all the good you can to the bodies and souls of men."[101] He kept in balance personal and social holiness. The call remains for the individual and the church to oppose persons and systems that are unholy. The mandate to liberate the captives is as much in force as ever, and the sanctifying grace of God makes such ministry possible.

Finally, Christian perfection is *an experience to grow in.* Wesley maintained that the experience was "improvable."[102]

[100]Jackson, *Works,* 11:395–96.
[101]Jackson, *Works,* 11:432.
[102]Jackson, *Works,* 11:442.

While it's been alluded to earlier, it needs to be emphasized on its own. With motives fixed, the Christian cooperates with the grace of God to close the gap between intention and performance. Not to do this would be to make a sham out of Christian perfection.

Another illustration from life can show how perfection can be developed and improved. When each of our children turned four years of age, they were "perfect" as far as the developmental charts were concerned. They could do everything a four-year-old was supposed to do. In that sense we could say, "We have a perfect four-year-old." But we never believed this was the end of it. We saw their perfection as a fact, but a fact laid against the larger need to continue on in the maturing process. In fact, their perfection at four years of age had within it the seeds of its own development.

Transferring this into the spiritual dimension, we can see how Wesley could speak of Christian perfection on the one hand and still exhort others to "go on to perfection." The critical factor in Christian perfection is the fixation of motive, the surrender of self-will. With this nailed down, the "perfect Christian" moves on to work out the implications of this commitment.

These then are some of the major dimensions of Christian perfection. These concepts caused Wesley to believe that God had raised up the people called Methodist to "spread scriptural holiness across the land."[103] He believed Methodism would remain vital only so long as it proclaimed this truth.[104]

This being so, it is necessary to consider the ongoing significance of Christian perfection. Perhaps as you have read you have thought of relevant associations between Wesley's

---

[103]Jackson, *Works,* 8:299.
[104]Jackson, *Works,* 4:83. Wesley expressed similar sentiments in his letters (see Telford, *Letters,* 4:321; 7:109).

views and your life. For me, the following points are evidences that this message is still needed in the Christian community.

First, Christian perfection maintains dynamism in Christian experience. Ours is a day when discipleship is being stressed. Wesley's theology is particularly relevant because it calls every believer to be growing. There is no room for relying on yesterday's experience, no matter how significant it was. One is always challenged to "go on to perfection." Nominal Christianity will not produce vigorous disciples. Only the deepest of commitments, continually renewed and expanded, will suffice. That is what Christian perfection calls for.

We do not go far in our walk with Christ before we are tempted to relax our devotion. We can come to believe that our past is sufficient to carry us through. Even in Wesley's day, people were looking to their baptism as infants as proof that they were Christians. Wesley cut through such attempts and called people to find "proof" in their present relationship with Christ.[105] Christian perfection counters the temptation to spiritual inertia. A vigorous proclamation of this truth can move many out of the doldrums and into the dynamic of daily discipleship, helping people sense a new depth of God's grace and a fresh realization of their importance in the kingdom.

Second, the doctrine of Christian perfection helps us face our struggles. I'm grateful to live in a time when we can share our needs openly in the body of Christ. This freedom and climate of concern have given new expression to *koinonia*. Wesley's doctrine of Christian perfection creates a theological avenue for this kind of sharing. Because we are accepted by God on the basis of our motives, we need not fear sharing our failures of performance. We can call our actions and attitudes by

---

[105]Jackson, *Works*, 6:73–76 (sermon: "The New Birth").

name. We do not have to rationalize or redefine what we are and what we do.

Unfortunately, some Christians (even some who believe in Christian perfection) have felt that admission of failure was tantamount to loss of the experience. Consequently, damaging emotions have been suppressed. Things like anger have been labeled "righteous indignation." Gossip has been spread in the name of "sharing prayer concerns." I've met Christians who have harbored all sorts of needs and guilt but have never felt the freedom to share for fear of judgment and rejection by their brothers and sisters in Christ. Thank God that a positive interpretation of Christian perfection *invites* the sharing of need. Honest confession becomes a doorway through which God's healing grace can flow.

Third, Christian perfection creates unity in life. We all know the tendency to live in compartments. We all wear several "hats" and find it difficult to juggle them sometimes. It's not uncommon to hear people express the feeling of being pulled in too many directions. When this becomes our norm for living, energy is dissipated. What a contrast to think that, while we never can eliminate actions and involvement, we can live for *one* purpose! We can have a controlling motive to live out all our roles for the glory of God and the service of others. It is difficult to grasp the importance of this until it is laid against contemporary emphases on self. Christian perfection calls for a radical *other-orientation*— toward God and neighbor. The irony is that it offers a depth of fulfillment that cannot be found through the various movements that focus on self-preoccupation.

Biblically, this is confirmed by David, who can accomplish much because he is a man after God's own heart. Paul can do all things through Christ who strengthens him. Psychologically, it is verified in the knowledge that an integrated personality can do more than one that is fragmented. Even our young people voice the truth when they exhort each other to "get it all together." The truth of unitive living is important today, and it is affirmed in the Christian faith by the doctrine of Christian perfection.

In the scientific realm, the laser beam illustrates Christian perfection's witness to the power of unitive living. In the laser beam, light is concentrated into a single beam that can penetrate the hardest substances known to man. As the diffused light is brought together into the single beam, tremendous power is generated. Wesley was saying the same thing: As more and more of our lives are harmonized around a central purpose, we experience greater and greater power.

Finally, Christian perfection points to a consummation. Life is going somewhere. Our perfection is not absolute in this life, but we believe there will come a day when it will be. We will exchange the perishable for the imperishable. Wesley's doctrine of Christian perfection is not an escape from reality, because it is firmly rooted in this life. But neither is it bound to this life. It contains the promise of future glory. We are on the way, and that way ends in God's house!

In short, the doctrine of Christian perfection raises our faith above the idea of religion as another "good cause" in society. All of us, whether followers of Jesus or not, are already up to our eyeballs in good causes. If Christianity is only one more to add to the list, then we can justifiably say no to it. But if Christianity is fundamentally different, that's another matter. If Christianity dares to speak of *transformation* of life in time and eternity in a way that affects all the "good causes," then that's different! The doctrine of Christian perfection makes this claim.

Questions for Reflection and Discussion

1. In your reading of the chapter, were any misconceptions about Christian perfection cleared up?
2. Which point of relevancy strikes you as being most important in your life, in the lives of those you know, and in the corporate life of the church?
3. Are there other significant relevancies that came to your mind as you read the chapter?

For Further Reading

"A Plain Account of Christian Perfection," in Jackson's *The Works of John Wesley*, 11:366–446.

Sermon: "Christian Perfection," in Jackson's *The Works of John Wesley*, 6:1–22.

Sermon: "Scriptural Christianity," in Jackson's *The Works of John Wesley*, 5:37–52.

Sermon: "The Repentance of Believers," in Jackson's *The Works of John Wesley*, 5:156–70.

Sermon: "The Great Privilege of Those That Are Born of God," in Jackson's *The Works of John Wesley*, 5:223–33.

Chapter Eight

THE END
OF THE JOURNEY
(GLORIFICATION)

This life is only a training ground
for the one that is to come.

COLIN W. WILLIAMS

7 If Christianity is to have significance, it must deal with eternal issues. The ultimate question on the lips of people is this: "Is this life all there is, or is there more?" This was true in Wesley's day, just as it is in ours. He wrote on one occasion that he wanted to know one thing—the way to heaven.[106] In one sense, his whole theology is an attempt to spell out that way.

Wesley would affirm what Colin Williams has written on this chapter's title page. He knew that what we are doing (or not doing) in this life shapes us for the life to come. With Keith Miller he would agree that heaven and hell are not so much rewards and punishments as they are consequences. Transformation is begun in this life. Because of that, important things can be said about the end of the journey, about our glorification.

First of all, the kingdom of God is here right now. We do not have to put the emphasis on some future climactic event outside the bounds of space and time as we know it. As Christians we affirm and look forward to existence in eternity, but we *live* in the present. In fact, I believe it can be said that Christians know how to live fully in the present because they have come to terms with eternity. We have come to see that the kingdom of God is in our midst right now. Wesley called the kingdom "heaven opened in the soul."[107] And he believed this occurs in this life.

But we do not believe we have experienced everything the kingdom has to offer us. There is a difference between "what is"

---

[106]Jackson, *Works*, 5:3.
[107]Jackson, *Works*, 5:81 (sermon: "The Way to the Kingdom").

and "what is to come." Added to our ability to live confidently in the present, then, is the ability to live hopefully with respect to the future. We do not dwell on "the sweet by-and-by," but we do look forward to the day when our commitment to Christ will not be encumbered by our sinfulness or the limitations of our humanity. We agree with the apostle Paul that there is coming a time when we will no longer see a poor reflection as in a mirror, but rather face to face (see 1 Corinthians 13:12).

But in the meantime we live fully in the present. In fact, Wesley spoke to this very thing when he said, "Your life is continued to you upon the earth for no other purpose than this, that you may know, love, and serve God on earth, and enjoy him to all eternity."[108] Wesley knew that we continually live with one foot in the "now" and the other foot in the "not yet." The kingdom is both present and future, but we are not pulled apart.

Second, the kingdom comes as an active presence. It is not neutral. The cross is ultimate proof of this truth. Wesley put it this way:

> The substance of all is, "Jesus Christ came into the world to save sinners"; or "God so loved the world, that he gave his only-begotten Son, to the end that we might not perish, but have everlasting life"; or "He was bruised for our transgressions, he was wounded for our iniquities, the chastisement of our peace was upon him; and with his stripes we are healed." Believe this and the Kingdom is thine.[109]

Because the kingdom has to be reckoned with as a presently active reality, we must come to terms one way or the other with it. The kingdom breaks through to call us to a decision of acceptance or rejection. Neutrality is not an option. In a sense, God

---

[108]Jackson, *Works*, 7:230 (sermon: "What Is Man?").
[109]Jackson, *Works*, 5:85.

has forced the issue by coming among us in Jesus Christ. All the rest of life is a response to this fact and the implications of it.

The issue of our ultimate glorification is based on the responses we make to the presence of the kingdom. It is the *activity* of the kingdom that makes a real connection between time and eternity. Like the ripple effect produced when a rock falls into the water, the decisions we make today carry over into our tomorrows. Life is not disjointed. Heaven and earth are connected by the way we live with regard to kingdom principles.

Third, not everyone is going to respond positively to the gospel message. Wesley knew that even though the kingdom was present and active, some people would decline the offer to live in it. He spoke of those "who, in spite of all the warnings of God, resolve to have their portion with the devil and his angels."[110] For these it would mean the loss of authentic existence here and now, but at the moment of death it meant an eternal loss.

On one occasion I had the opportunity to be part of a local church's study of the book of Revelation. A guest minister was invited to bring the overview presentation for the study. Near the end of his address he said, "One of the reasons I'm a United Methodist is because John Wesley was a universalist—he believed everyone was going to be saved."

Let there be no misunderstanding; let it be said emphatically that nothing could be farther from the truth. It is true that Wesley believed salvation was offered to everyone. He did believe everyone *could* be saved, but he never believed that all people *would* be saved. He knew that some people would always prefer darkness to light. Wesley derived no pleasure in proclaiming the reality of eternal death, but he held to the truth as he believed it to be set forth in Scripture. His own words are indicative of that: "Knowest thou not that the wages of sin is death?—death, not

---

[110]Jackson, *Works*, 6:382 (sermon: "Of Hell").

only temporal, but eternal. . . . This is the sentence, to be punished with never-ending death, with everlasting destruction from the presence of the Lord, and from the glory of his power."[111]

As he deemed it appropriate, Wesley urged people to give up the notion that they could remain in their sin and still go to heaven. He told them to be done with any ideas that they could make personal atonement for their sins and thereby "deserve" heaven. He was realistic enough to know that the presence of the kingdom demands a verdict, because it passes judgment on the sinfulness of humanity. This "dark side" of the kingdom message shows that the call to salvation is neither nonsense nor sentimentality. The reality of eternal separation from the presence of God makes the gospel more sobering, real, and urgent. This reality was one of the factors that moved Wesley to do everything humanly possible to win men and women to Christ.

Fourth, the positive aspects of kingdom living outweigh the negative dimensions. While Wesley fully accepted the New Testament doctrine of hell, he *emphasized* the grace and love of God. He believed that this was a more powerful motivation to commitment than fear or threat of punishment. Consequently, he went about preaching the glad tidings of salvation, offering people Christ as Savior from sin and Giver of life! In the conference minutes of 1746 he included a statement about overemphasizing the wrath of God. He said that such preaching "generally hardens them that believe not, and discourages them that do."[112] So he preferred to call people to Christ on the basis of love.

At first glance this seems to fit right in with our contemporary emphasis on love. Even in the church there is the emphasis on being loving and affirming. But the contemporary interpretation of love and Wesley's understanding of love part company

---

[111]Jackson, *Works*, 5:83.
[112]Albert Outler, *John Wesley* (New York: Oxford Press, 1964), 163.

at one point—*accountability*. The all-embracing notions of love today include little or no accountability and make no calls for change. This makes a call to repentance and confession of sin seem antiquated and narrow-minded. People say, "If you really loved us, you would not judge us." Wesley would respond, "It is precisely because I *do* love you that I call you to repent of your sins and align yourself with the will and way of God." The Wesley way is the way of love, and we must be forever glad about that. But it is a love that confronts sin and calls for change. God's love accepts us as we are, but it does not leave us as we are.

Every day as a parent I love my children. I love them to the depths of my soul. But sometimes this love calls them into accountability. Sometimes my love calls for change. There are times when my love is not all-accepting, for to do so would be to affirm unacceptable behavior. So parental love seeks to operate in such a way that my children will grow to be responsible adults. Uncritical, "blind" love would end up producing irresponsibility. Wesley serves us well at the point of making love preeminent, but not to the extent that it overlooks sin and ends up condoning the very things that will destroy what it means to be human.

Given the ideas that have already been shared, Wesley could turn his eye toward heaven and look to a glorious consummation in Christ:

> [God will give] an unmixed state of holiness and happiness, far superior to that which Adam enjoyed in Paradise. . . . "God shall wipe away all tears from their eyes; and there shall be no more death, neither sorrow nor crying; Neither shall there be any more pain; for the former things are done away!" As there will be no more death and no more pain or sickness preparatory thereto; as there

will be no more grieving for, or parting with, friends; so there will be no more sorrow or crying. Nay, but there will be a greater deliverance than all this; for there will be no more sin. And, to crown all, there will be a deep, intimate, uninterrupted union with God; a constant communion with the Father and his Son Jesus Christ, through the Spirit; a continual enjoyment of the Three-One God, and of all the creatures in him![113]

Here is one of the strengths of Wesley's theology: It has a word for eternity, but it is a word that does not divide it from time. The word for the end of the journey (and beyond) is only a climax to the word for the start of the journey and its progress. The life we live now we live by faith in Jesus Christ, and this alone paves the way for the unspeakable joys of heaven.

Perhaps the greatest test of anyone's theology is its ability to sustain him or her in the hour of death. In his earlier days Wesley had been plagued by the fear of death. At critical times in his life it had risen up to render him useless. But as he grew in his understanding of glorification and its relation to life here and now, he matured in this area. By holding together the connectedness of time and eternity, Wesley was able to end his life with words that describe the Christian relationship to time and eternity. Just before he experienced glorification in its ultimate sense, he uttered these simple words: "The best of all is, God is with us!"

Questions for Reflection and Discussion

1. In what ways (verbally and nonverbally) do you see people struggling with the question of eternal life?

---

[113]Jackson, *Works*, 6:295–96 (sermon: "The New Creation").

2. How does an awareness of our purpose here on earth help settle the question of eternal life?
3. Do you agree that the motive of love is a stronger incentive to commitment than fear? Why?
4. How can the church recover a message of love that still calls for accountability and change? Why do so many see love and accountability as opposites?

For Further Reading

Sermon: "The Great Assize," in Jackson's *The Works of John Wesley,* 5:171–84.

Sermon: "Upon Our Lord's Sermon on the Mount," Discourse VII, in Jackson's *The Works of John Wesley,* 5:344–60.

Sermon: "Upon Our Lord's Sermon on the Mount," Discourse XI, in Jackson's *The Works of John Wesley,* 5:405–12.

Sermon: "On Eternity," in Jackson's *The Works of John Wesley,* 6:189–98.

Sermon: "Of Hell," in Jackson's *The Works of John Wesley,* 6:381–91.

Sermon: "On the Resurrection of the Dead," in Jackson's *The Works of John Wesley,* 7:474–84.

Chapter Nine

ALL TOGETHER NOW
(THE CHURCH)

---

*Wesley understood that the concept of the church
was at stake in his reforming mission.*

HOWARD SNYDER

Strictly speaking we have completed our examination of Wesley's "order of salvation," but we have not fully described his theology. If we stopped here, we would miss one of his most important emphases—the church. Wesley was first, last, and always a *churchman* in the finest sense of the term. He lived and died a clergyman in the Church of England. He believed that authentic Christian experience had to be nurtured in community. He cared little for solitary religion. In the next two chapters we must examine his views as they relate to the church. In this chapter we'll look at Wesley's theology of the church; in the next we'll consider his views in relation to church renewal.

In a time when mainline denominations are floundering, it is not easy to promote a doctrine of the church. All over the country I meet those who see the church more as a hindrance than a help. The late Quaker scholar D. Elton Trueblood described the mood by saying, "The hardest problem of Christianity is the problem of the church. We cannot live with it, and we cannot live without it."[114] The result is a rise in parachurch organizations, which have become substitute churches for many. Surveys conducted by pollsters such as George Barna and George Gallup Jr. confirm that more people profess a born-again experience than can be found actively participating in the churches of our land.

---

[114]Cited in Frank Bateman Stanger, "Christ Is Building His Church," *The Herald* (Asbury Theological Seminary) 94, no. 1 (1982): 18.

Such conditions are not as far removed from Wesley as we might first think. In the early eighteenth century, institutional religion was largely in eclipse. Spirituality was often promoted by independent and separatist groups. A personally assured faith was often labeled as enthusiasm. When the Evangelical Revival began, Wesley could easily have formed his followers into another denomination, but he didn't. Instead, he remained consciously in the Church of England and sought to revive it from within.[115] When the Methodists were accused of promoting schism in the Anglican Church, Wesley replied that he and his followers held "communion therewith in the same manner as they did twenty years ago, and hope to do so until the end of their lives."[116]

All this is to show that a doctrine of the church was important to John Wesley. But the question arises, "What is the church?" In Wesley's own day various answers were given. Some equated it with the building. Others defined it within the limits of a particular denomination. Wesley preferred a more general and, in his belief, a more biblical idea. He called the church "a body of people united together in the service of God."[117] As we'll see, he amplified this definition to give it more precise meaning, but his intention was to say that the church is *personal*. He felt that to lose this understanding was to lose the biblical view of the church.

At the same time, Wesley was a realist. Even though he had a broad definition of the church, he knew people would naturally group themselves into particular denominations.[118] He

---

[115]*The Appeal to Men of Reason and Religion* and *The Farther Appeal to Men of Reason and Religion* are Wesley's most comprehensive attempts to defend Methodism's place in the Church of England. See Jackson, *Works,* 8:1–247.

[116]Outler, *John Wesley,* 172.

[117]Jackson, *Works,* 6:392 (sermon: "Of the Church").

[118]Jackson, *Works,* 6:392–93. Cf. Outler, *John Wesley,* 172.

didn't judge this to be wrong; he didn't try to eliminate distinctions between denominations. The unity he saw and worked for was more a *unity of spirit* than a unity of structure. Consequently, he had friends and supporters in a wide range of communions. He could move easily among groups as diverse as Roman Catholics and independents, which was due, in the end, to his fundamental understanding of the church as people.

It is still this personal dimension that attracts people to the church. Surveys are confirming that most people today are drawn toward the church because of its personal emphases—relational ministries, warm and friendly atmosphere, meaningful fellowship, and setting in which significant friendships can be formed. Sadly, though, too many churches lack the personal dimension. Institutionalism sometimes takes precedence over individuals. Buildings and budgets can seem to be more important than ultimate concerns. These emphases create a psychology that views the church more as an organization than an organism. When this happens, we've lost the foundational attitude that was so important to Wesley.

Wesley affirmed the personal dimension, using Ephesians 4:1–6 as his controlling text—a passage emphasizing the unity of believers. With Paul, Wesley saw the church as one body, "comprehending not only ... any one family, not only the Christians of one congregation, of one city, of one province, or nation, but all persons on the face of the earth who answer the character here given."[119] In other words, he believed in the church universal.

Even when the Methodist movement gained momentum, Wesley continued to maintain that his followers were nothing more than Bible Christians. He resolutely stated that they did not divide themselves at all from the living body of Christ, or even

---

[119]Jackson, *Works*, 6:394.

from the Church of England.[120] At the same time he did not lose the priority of God's will over the opinions and organizations of men. He wrote, "We will obey the rules and governors of the Church whenever we can, consistently with our duty of God. Whenever we cannot, we will quietly obey God rather than men."[121] This spirit enabled Wesley to exercise an ecumenical spirit, all the while seeking God's will above any human associations. In the final analysis, this is what it means to say that the church is one body.

Wesley also affirmed that the church has one Spirit. For him it was the Spirit who "animates . . . all the living members of the Church of God."[122] This idea is crucial, for it makes it plain that Wesley did not equate membership in a church with spiritual vitality. Early in his ministry he encountered those who equated membership and experience. Sermons like "The Circumcision of the Heart" and "Salvation by Faith" fell on stony ground. But Wesley went on, knowing that the Holy Spirit was the "fountain of all spiritual life."[123]

It is important to note that Wesley did not advocate any particular manifestation of the Spirit as necessary proof that one was Spirit-filled. His journal documents many extraordinary (even unusual) manifestations.[124] Interestingly, Wesley did not seek to promote or prohibit such occurrences. He was aware that some experiences were counterfeit, but he knew that many were authentic. Time would reveal which were which. In the rapid pace of his ministry Wesley did not feel called to spend an

---

[120]One of Wesley's clearest statements to this effect was "The Character of a Methodist," *Works*, 8:339–47. The conference minutes of 1747 also contain comments of a similar nature; see Outler, *John Wesley*, 172.

[121]Outler, *John Wesley*, 173.

[122]Jackson, *Works*, 6:394.

[123]Jackson, *Works*, 6:394.

[124]Jackson, *Works*, 1:187–97. The first two months (April and May 1739) of Wesley's field preaching serve as a good example of such manifestations.

inordinate amount of time judging the response and experience of his hearers.

In our own time the charismatic renewal has matured in this regard. In the earlier days people seemed quite consumed with judging the validity or invalidity of others' experiences. In more recent times the emphasis has switched from particular gifts to the powerful Giver of the gifts. Wesley would rejoice in this. He knew that God works in many ways his wonders to perform. One of the dynamics of revival is that it breaks through stereotypes and deals with people individually. Wesley would call us to promote the Spirit-filled life, but without passing judgment on how such a life is to be lived.

Allowing that the church is one body made alive by the one Spirit, Wesley went on to declare that it has one Lord, one faith, and one baptism. For Wesley, the lordship of Christ is the Christian's greatest joy. To live under this lordship provides an experience that he could only describe as "sitting in heavenly places with Christ."[125] But it was not sitting in the passive sense of the term. Christ's lordship calls for our *disciplined obedience*. This is one reason why Wesley emphasized the means of grace. He knew that personally and corporately we are called to live under Christ's lordship. No area is outside of his control.

When Wesley said that the church has one faith, he did not mean a single code of doctrine to which all were bound to subscribe. His own theological position included an indebtedness to Roman Catholic, Lutheran, Reformed, Puritan, and Anglican traditions.[126] In this sense Methodism has always recognized a healthy breadth in belief. The chief criterion for entrance into

---

[125]Jackson, *Works*, 6:394.

[126]One of the best works to demonstrate Wesley's indebtedness to a variety of theological traditions is Colin Williams's *John Wesley's Theology Today* (Nashville: Abingdon, 1960).

the united societies was not a particular theological stance but "a desire to flee from the wrath to come."[127]

Unfortunately, this spirit has been taken to mean that Methodists are theologically indifferent. Wesley's statement "If thy heart is right as my heart is right, give me thy hand" has been mistakenly used to support contemporary, open-ended pluralism. However, to interpret him this way makes at least three mistakes: (1) it overlooks the fact that reputable Wesley scholars have borne witness to his classic orthodoxy,[128] (2) it forgets that Wesley himself stood against trends toward uncritical pluralism[129] in his own day, and (3) it blurs the distinction between doctrine and opinion. When Wesley urged his followers to have a "catholic spirit," it is clear from the context that he meant in matters that were nonessential.[130] In the same sermon, in fact, he spoke to those who would equate catholic spirit with open-ended pluralism: "A man of truly catholic spirit has not now his religion to seek. He is fixed as the sun in his judgment concerning the main branches of Christian doctrine. . . . He does not halt between two opinions or vainly try to blend them into one."[131]

When Wesley said that the church has one faith, he did not have an ambiguous concept of faith in mind. He believed that the fundamental doctrines of Christianity were set forth in Scripture, articulated in the major creeds of the first 450 years of church history,[132] and described in the Anglican Church's

---

[127]John Wesley, *The Nature, Design, and General Rules of the United Societies* (Newcastle-Upon-Tyne: John Gooding on the Side, 1743), 5. Cf. Jackson, *Works,* 8:270.

[128]Outler, *John Wesley,* 92. Cf. Williams, *John Wesley's Theology Today,* 13–17.

[129]The term for this in the eighteenth century was "speculative latitudinarianism." Wesley stood against this. Cf. Jackson, *Works,* 8:214.

[130]Jackson, *Works,* 5:492–504 (sermon: "Catholic Spirit").

[131]Jackson, *Works,* 5:492–504.

[132]Especially the Apostles' and Nicene Creeds.

"Thirty-nine Articles of Religion." This accounts for his not producing another creed for the early Methodists in Britain. Rupert Davies correctly notes that "Wesley, as a practical man, did not spend time in expounding what had been perfectly well expounded by others."[133] But let there be no doubt that he knew and accepted classic orthodoxy. That he wanted others to do the same is clear, especially in relation to American Methodists. When it became clear that the American Methodists would form a separate denomination, Wesley showed his concern for content in faith by abridging the thirty-nine articles of the Church of England into twenty-four statements of faith that he expected the new church to embrace.[134]

The real question for Wesley on the matter of faith was not content but the question "How does faith operate in the church?" For some it operated as a test. Persons were admitted into the fellowship of some churches only if they accepted the particular statement of faith held by that body. For Wesley, faith was first of all *awareness*. It was characterized early on by repentance. Adherence to the group's doctrine came later, after faith (as turning from sin to Christ) was professed. Wesley operated on the premise that faith must first be existential before it can be conceptual. In this he felt he was following the example of the early church, which developed its creeds as an expression of its faith, not a precondition for it. He also thought that this approach would guard against *creedalism* and the "dead orthodoxy" that had characterized too many groups of his day.

This faith was confirmed in "one baptism." Theologically, Wesley saw baptism as bestowing grace, which cleansed one of the guilt of original sin and opened the way to a future of faith

---

[133]Rupert Davies, *Methodism* (London: Epworth, 1963), 82.

[134]These articles can be found in the Book of Discipline of denominations associated with early Methodism—the United Methodist, Free Methodist, Wesleyan Methodist, and Nazarene churches.

and hope in Christ.[135] He saw it not only as a single act, but also as the sign to the church that God is continually bestowing grace upon the body.[136] Wesley didn't try to explain how this is done. He was wise enough to leave mystery as mystery, but he did want his people to see baptism as more than a mere symbol. He wanted them to see it as an actual means of grace, as a genuine act of God in the life of the one baptized.

As we have seen, Wesley followed closely the Pauline analogy of the church in the book of Ephesians. He felt that this was the biblical answer to the question "What is the church?" He also believed that Paul's description was harmonious with the nineteenth article of religion in the Anglican Church, which states, "The visible Church of Christ is a congregation of faithful men, in which the pure word of God is preached, and the sacraments be duly administered."[137]

Wesley recognized that to be this kind of body placed weighty responsibilities on its members, which is why discipline was so important to him in the growth of the Methodist societies. Using Scripture again, he identified these tasks with living a life "worthy of the calling you have received" (Ephesians 4:1). This meant thinking, speaking, and acting in *every instance* in a manner worthy of Christ. Specifically, it meant adopting a spirit of humility and love, striving for the unity of the Spirit through the bond of peace.[138]

Wesley's own words are the best way to summarize his views of the church. Realizing that the church is God's primary vehicle for extending the kingdom until Christ returns, this is what Wesley wrote:

---

[135]Jackson, *Works,* 10:188–201.
[136]Jackson, *Works,* 6:395.
[137]Jackson, *Works,* 6:396.
[138]Jackson, *Works,* 6:398–99.

In the mean time, let all those who are real members of the Church, see that they walk holy and unblamable in all things. "Ye are the light of the world!" Ye are "a city set upon a hill" and "cannot be hid." O "let your light shine before men!" Show them your faith by your works. Let them see, by the whole tenor of your conversation, that your hope is all laid up above! Let all your words and actions evidence the spirit whereby you are animated! Above all things, let your love abound. Let it extend to every child of man: Let it overflow to every child of God. By this let all men know whose disciples ye are, because you "love one another."[139]

Questions for Reflection and Discussion

1. What light does Wesley's decision to remain within the Church of England shed on contemporary efforts at church renewal?

2. How do you respond to Wesley's fundamental notion of the church as *personal?* Why does it strike you the way it does?

3. How can Wesley's response to differing Christian experiences be a guide for us? Is it sufficient to simply let time show what is authentic and what is not? What other criteria, if any, would you want to add?

4. In an age of pluralism it's not easy to have an open spirit and a clear commitment to orthodoxy. How can the Wesleyan emphasis here be applied today? In your experience, which side of the coin needs more emphasis—openness of spirit or commitment to orthodoxy? Why?

---

[139]Jackson, *Works*, 6:400–401.

For Further Reading

Sermon: "Of the Church," in Jackson's *The Works of John Wesley*, 6:392–401.

Sermon: "On Schism," in Jackson's *The Works of John Wesley*, 6:401–10.

Sermon: "On Attending the Church Service," in Jackson's *The Works of John Wesley*, 6:174–85.

Almost the whole of volume 10 of *The Works of John Wesley* is devoted to Wesley's view of the church and the place of the early Methodist movement in the larger body of Christ.

Chapter Ten

VISION AND MEANS

*When viewed with excitement as the whole gospel
for the whole person and as energized by the Spirit
of God, this vision will surely renew the church
to the glory of God and to the salvation of many.*

LACEYE WARNER

Theology never exists in a vacuum. It arises in response to a particular vision expressing itself through specific applications in a particular time and place. The vision describes the theologian's sense of God's revelation, and the application has to do with the ways in which the vision is lived out individually and in community—both in the church and in the world. Theology often transcends the theologian's life span and location, but it can never be divorced from it.

Wesley's message is no exception. His understanding of the gospel is rooted in the vision that inspired him, and it is reflected in the early Methodist movement that shaped people into the image of Christ. The way to heaven was a way that blended the supernatural and the natural. It was a way that moved people from sin to salvation and developed them into authentic and vital disciples. The preceding chapters have focused on Wesley's message. In this chapter we turn our attention to the vision and means that accompanied it.[140] We will see how the vision defined the message and how the means Wesley used expressed the mission and fulfilled the vision.

More than anything else, Wesley's vision of theology as "the way to heaven" was *transformational*. The gospel is about a life

---

[140]I did not see this connection between vision, message, and means as clearly as I should have in the first edition in 1983. This has been one of the significant learnings for me in the ensuing twenty years. I now see Wesley's entire theology and ministry as a unified whole, and I believe that he operated with this sense as well. This may help explain why he used "the order of salvation" as his system rather than the traditional topical approach.

radically changed by an encounter with Christ and a life lived in Christ and for Christ. One of his favorite texts was Galatians 2:20—"I am crucified with Christ: and I live no longer, but Christ liveth in me: and the life that I now live in the flesh I live by faith in the Son of God, who loved me and delivered himself up for me."[141] These words captured the deliverance from sin that cleansed one's inner being and empowered one's outward conduct. The result was nothing less than "a new creation" (2 Corinthians 5:17). The grand vision of Wesley's theology was Christ living in the believer, bringing all that is holy, just, and good.[142]

This vision was for *all*. Wesley stood against the Roman Catholic idea of a special spirituality for the religious (priests, monks, and nuns), and he rejected the Calvinistic doctrine of election as double predestination.[143] At the same time, he soundly denied any notion of universalism, keeping the doctrine of salvation by faith fully intact. His vision was one of God—the God who is not willing that any should perish but that all should come to salvation (see 2 Peter 3:9). In whatever way it did not happen, the fault did not lie in the nature and activity of God, but rather in the nature and activity of people. But more important, it meant that God's offer of salvation was extended to everyone. Consequently, soteriology was at the heart of Wesley's theology, and his entire message and methods were an "order of salvation."

Second, the vision was necessarily *missiological*. God's love for the whole world and the plan to save anyone through Jesus

---

[141]Wesley, *Explanatory Notes Upon the New Testament*, 685.

[142]Jackson, *Works*, 11:377 (treatise: "A Plain Account of Christian Perfection").

[143]Jackson, *Works*, 10:204–59 (treatise: "Predestination Calmly Considered"). Several other treatises relate to this theme, immediately following this one just cited. For more on Wesley's views regarding election, see my chapter in *Four Views on Eternal Security* (Grand Rapids: Zondervan, 2002), 209–55.

(see John 3:16) could not be contained within an individual's personal experience. God saves us one at a time but not in isolation or without responsibility for others. Even though Wesley experienced his heart "strangely warmed," and even though he understood the gospel to be a "religion of the heart," he abhorred any notion that such faith could remain privatized.[144] Consequently, his vision was of the gospel expressing itself in a life of compassion and service—"faith working by love," as he so often called it.

Although the works of God were many, Wesley believed that the missiological nature of the gospel expressed itself in three primary movements—regeneration of the lost, renewal of the church, and reform of the nation.[145] While it is possible to see each of these elements finding their own expression in Wesley's life and work, most often they were found in some combination. For example, he did not hesitate to call members of the Church of England to be regenerated. He never believed that church membership alone was sufficient for salvation. He also linked the reform of the nation to the renewal of the church, sharing with many others the belief that the church was the nation's conscience. The grand outcome of successful efforts in these three areas would be to "spread scriptural holiness" across the land.

But even here, Wesley was not being original. Rather, he was placing Methodism in the stream of the larger, historic holy-living tradition.[146] His own experience of this tradition and its influence is clearly seen in his reading lists and in the works he

---

[144]For more on Wesley's concept of "religion of the heart," see Greg Clapper's *As If the Heart Mattered* (Nashville: Upper Room, 1997).

[145]George G. Hunter III, *To Spread the Power* (Nashville: Abingdon, 1987), 40.

[146]See Outler, *John Wesley*, and Richard Foster, *Streams of Living Water* (San Francisco: HarperSanFrancisco, 1998).

urged others to read.[147] He could not conceive of any theology separated from holiness of heart and life—God's grace transforming our inner character and directing our outward conduct. In the finest sense of the word, "the way to heaven" is about making saints, and this cannot be done without a theology that is intensely ethical.

Such was the essence of Wesley's vision. It was never a static, once-for-all view of God and God's will. It was, more accurately, theology worked out over time and in relation to actual circumstances. But standing behind the daily living out of the gospel was Wesley's firm and unwavering belief in the providence of God.

As we are about to see, though, Wesley's vision could not be realized without specific means for achieving it. His methods are as important as the vision that gave rise to them. Because this is a theological view of Wesley's message, we must return once more to his primary understanding of the gospel as an "order of salvation." The flow of grace (prevenient, converting, sanctifying, and glorifying) was akin to the Johannine understanding of "waves of grace" (see John 1:16) operating unceasingly across the human journey. Once we see this, we hold the key to interpreting "the way to heaven"—the gospel according to Wesley. But the conceptual or theoretical nature of such interpretation is only half the story—which we've examined in the main portion of this book. The part we want to focus on now is the practical, ministry-based dimensions.[148]

---

[147]I dealt extensively with these reading lists in my Ph.D. dissertation at Duke University—*The Devotional Life of John Wesley: 1703–38* (Ann Arbor, Mich.: University Microfilms, 1981).

[148]Since writing *John Wesley's Message for Today* in 1983, I have come to see the connection between Wesley's theological categories and his primary ministry expressions. In a very real sense, his "theological genius" lies squarely in his connection of belief and practice—doctrine and ministry.

John Wesley was a "folk theologian."[149] Yet even this term has misled some who read him mistakenly. They would interpret this phrase to justify an immediate watering down of Wesley's theological content. But that would be an incorrect interpretation. Rather, to say that Wesley was a folk theologian means that he could not remain content with "speculative theology"—that is, theology that ends with the formation of ideas—theology that is topical rather than transformational. His emphasis was on "practical divinity," a message with both solid content and an actual outworking in life. For Wesley, theology that fails to achieve this cannot be called good theology. The life of God in the human soul (see Colossians 1:27) is the final test of any theology.

This leads directly to the first means to be noted—Wesley's connection of theological content to a ministry structure. In chapter 6, I briefly described the primary groups that comprised Methodism: the societies, classes, and bands. In actuality, these different associations were an expression of the "order of salvation." For each wave of grace, there was a corresponding formative element to connect people to that grace. It is not an exaggeration to say that every major theological concept has a home in some dimension of Methodism. This conscious alignment is one of Wesley's finest legacies to the Christian tradition.

At its broadest expression, the church served to span the entire spectrum and overshadow the whole journey. Even though Wesley viewed Methodism as an *ecclesiola en ecclesia,* he never saw it as a substitute church or as separate from the church.[150] The church was always the chief expression of the body of Christ—God's

---

[149]This term is usually attributed to Albert Outler, who used it in many of his writings about Wesley. It is now generally used among Wesley scholars to differentiate his message from one that is based in the academy.

[150]*Ecclesiola en ecclesia* means "the little church in the big church." It is essentially a renewal concept akin to the biblical idea of yeast in the dough. Just as yeast loses itself in the dough, so also does the little church give itself for the sake of edifying the big church.

primary expression of formative community. Yet within it, there was a need for other elements of structure to represent the gospel story—to promote the theology of grace and to nurture people accordingly.

To represent prevenient grace, Wesley used the united *societies*. To promote converting grace, he developed the *class* meeting. And to advance sanctifying grace, he emphasized the *band* meetings. The point here is not to describe these groups in detail but rather to show how each theological concept is matched by a corresponding ministry expression. The way to heaven is a journey from birth to death—a journey that combines supernatural power with structural reality. The divine story and the human experience are always in a dynamic relationship through a concrete ministry form.

Within this structural reality, we see the second means for Wesley, namely, leadership by devoted laity. Wesley was a priest in the Church of England, and whenever he could, he made use of other clergypersons to help him. But by and large, early Methodism was sustained by the laity. Wesley's vision to "offer them Christ" was carried out by devoted men and women who led the societies, classes, and bands. Wesley's theology of the priesthood of all believers was clearly expressed in the early Methodist movement. His vision for Methodists to "watch over one another in love" was achieved day by day through the compassion and acts of charity of laypeople all over England, Ireland, Scotland, and Wales.

Not surprisingly, Wesley did not leave such leadership to chance. He provided instruction for the laity, both in the conceptual and missional vision (for example, "The Character of a Methodist") and in the functional tasks related to leadership (for example, "The General Rules of the United Societies"). He reinforced his basic training with regular visits to the societies, often staying in the homes of the leaders and doubtless having constructive and intriguing conversations with them. Beyond that, he published an array of resources to assist leaders in their work—most especially *Explanatory Notes Upon the New Testament* (1755) and *Explanatory Notes Upon the Old Testament* (1765). This four-volume set provided the biblical base for the ongoing exposition of Scripture in the Methodist meetings—something Wesley believed to be essential if people were to know and follow the whole counsel of God. Had he not engaged in such painstaking efforts, the leaders would have been hampered in their ability to provide what was needed.

This emphasis on and use of lay leadership leads directly to the third key in his means—an ecumenical alliance to achieve the vision. Because early Methodism was a movement and not a denomination, no one had to leave his or her church in order to be a Methodist. For much of his life, Wesley saw to it that the Methodist meetings did not conflict with the worship hours of the churches.[151] This single fact reveals the depth of Wesley's commitment to the renewal of the church.

Methodism was barely a year old when he communicated this in a seminal essay titled "The Character of a Methodist."[152] In many ways it was the keynote for describing the kind of person who could properly be called a Methodist. Wesley highlighted these characteristics: a person (1) who has the love of God shed abroad in his heart by the Holy Ghost, (2) who is happy in God, (3) who has the hope of everlasting life, (4) who prays without ceasing, (5) who shows his love for God by loving his neighbors, (6) who seeks only to do God's will, (7) who

---

[151]This practice changed nearer to the end of his life as more and more churches reacted against Methodism, sometimes excluding "Methodists" from the sacrament of the Lord's Supper. The need to avoid overlap diminished, but Wesley *never intended* for Methodism to be a substitute church.

[152]Jackson, *Works*, 8:340–47.

manifests the fruit of the Spirit, (8) who keeps the commandments, (9) who never lives without accountability, and (10) who
does good to all men.

Nearly every characteristic is drawn directly from a Bible
verse, and all of them are nothing other than basic Christianity.
And that was precisely the point. Near the end of the treatise
he noted that readers would say, "Why, these are only the common fundamentals of Christianity!"

We can almost see Wesley smiling in the text itself. For he
meant to describe nothing other than "plain old Christianity." A
Methodist would never be distinguished by any more or less
than that. And again, such a definition was Christocentric in that
a Methodist would be one who had "the mind that was in Christ,
[who] walks as Christ also walked."[153]

This view enabled Methodism to reach out to "all the
people" in ways other movements and churches did not.[154]
People with no previous Christian experience and those who
had been members of churches for decades were equal
candidates for the establishment and nurture of true Christian
faith. Ironically, this approach made enemies as well as friends.
Because Wesley did not equate life in Christ with either polite
society or church membership, he both attracted those who
were hungry for God and repelled those who felt themselves
to be full enough.

In time, those who had become Christians through Methodist
witness rose to become leaders in the movement. Within the
ranks we can see people who directed Methodism while remain-
ing Anglicans, Presbyterians, Quakers, Puritans, and so forth.
This "kingdom alliance" gave Methodism a breadth and depth it

[153]Jackson, *Works*, 8:346.
[154]Lovett H. Weems Jr., *Leadership in the Wesleyan Spirit* (Nashville: Abingdon, 1999), 13.

would not have had through any single tradition. It also provided the Methodist meetings with a genuine spirit of hospitality greater than that of a denominationally limited fellowship.

The alliance can be further seen in the resources Wesley used to train leaders and nurture followers. His own personal reading list shows that he fed his soul on writers from Roman Catholicism, Eastern Orthodoxy, Lutheranism, Calvinism, and Puritanism—to name a few. Perhaps most of all, the multivolume *Christian Library,* published between 1749 and 1755, showed how much he wanted the early Methodists to feast on "the choicest pieces of practical divinity" drawn from a broad spectrum of Christian sources.[155] In all these ways, nothing less than a kingdom perspective would suffice.

Wesley's theology as a way to heaven had a compelling vision fueling it and concrete means advancing it. The vision was a lifelong journey of ever-increasing conformity to Christ, and the means were ministry groups designed to promote the life of God in the human soul. Richard Heitzenrater summarized the Wesleyan heritage as "the story of a people struggling together to understand God and themselves as they move from birth to death, from new birth to eternal life, from fear to joy, from doubt to confidence."[156] Wesley's passion in this regard enflamed his life and ministry for more than five decades, bringing him to his deathbed convinced that "the best of all is, God is with us!"

---

[155]John Wesley, *A Christian Library,* 50 volumes (Bristol, Tenn.: Felix Farley, 1749–55).

[156]Richard Heitzenrater, *Wesley and the People Called Methodists* (Nashville: Abingdon, 1995), 321.

Questions for Reflection and Discussion

1. Consider each element of Wesley's vision and means in relation to your own life. Which element in each category is most important to you right now? Why is this so?
2. Consider each element of Wesley's vision and means in relation to your church. Which element in each category is most important for your congregation right now? Why is this so?
3. Use the closing quotation by Richard Heitzenrater as a way of understanding life together in the body of Christ. What words stand out as particularly significant as you seek to discover God's vision and to implement this vision through discerned means?

For Further Reading

Wesley published his writings as one means to confirm that Methodism was indeed a valid work of God. To that extent, we may read his sermons, letters, and treatises as further documentation of his vision and means. But in particular, volume 8 of *The Works of John Wesley* contains the substantive documents that defined and directed the early Methodist movement:

"A Plain Account of the People Called Methodists"
"The General Rules of the United Societies"
"Rules of the Band-Societies"
"Minutes of Conversations between the Rev. Mr. Wesley and Others"
"Minutes of Several Conversations between the Rev. Mr. Wesley and Others"

"The Character of a Methodist"
"A Short History of Methodism"
"Advice to the People Called Methodists"
"The Principles of a Methodist"

Chapter Eleven

REGENERATION, RENEWAL, AND REFORM

A new look at the eighteenth-century period of renewal in the church's history could shed some light on the need that we face in the church today.

SAMUEL EMERICK

John Wesley was a true son of the Reformation. He would affirm with Martin Luther and John Calvin that the church is continually being renewed. He believed that Methodism was one of the primary means God had ordained in the eighteenth century to bring revival to the church.[157] We can be sure that he would support contemporary efforts at church renewal, and he'd want those in the Wesleyan tradition to be in the forefront of such concerns.

As we've seen, Wesley envisioned a threefold mission for Methodism: regeneration, renewal, and reform. Because his primary arena was the church, he saw its renewal as essential, and in some ways antecedent, to personal regeneration or societal reform. For him (and others), the church was the nation's conscience, and as such, it had to be healthy and active if the other two purposes were to be achieved. Consequently, church renewal was always in Wesley's heart as the catalyst for fulfilling the total mission God had given to the Methodists.

However, the questions remain, "What kind of renewal are we seeking, and how can we know if we are on the right track?" It is my conviction that we can learn much from John Wesley in the whole matter of church renewal.[158] In chapter 9 we looked at Wesley's doctrine of the church. We saw its central place in his theology and in his understanding of how people are nurtured

---

[157]Jackson, *Works*, 8:299.
[158]See Howard Snyder, *The Radical Wesley and Patterns for Church Renewal* (Downers Grove, Ill.: InterVarsity Press, 1980).

in their faith. But Wesley did not find himself in a church that exemplified the qualities it should. Consequently, he sought to design the early Methodist movement as a means for renewing the Church of England in particular and the larger body of Christ in general. We can detect key actions in his strategy for renewal.

First, he would urge all people to *personally experience Christ*. It had not been without intense struggle that Wesley came to see the centrality of a personal faith in Christ. His "heart-warming" experience at Aldersgate became the motivating purpose of his life. Justification by faith became the touchstone of the Methodist revival, and Wesley preached this theme on every conceivable occasion.[159]

Believing as he did in the necessity of personal faith, Wesley urged it on persons who were already members of the Church of England. To his surprise, the message fell on deaf ears. To them the notion of personally experiencing God smacked of "enthusiasm."[160] So pulpits began closing to him. But rather than compromise what he knew to be scriptural truth, Wesley continued to preach it. He moved into the open air and preached "the glad tidings of salvation" to those who were open to the message. It was in this context that the revival began—and the theme of personal salvation was its hallmark.

It seems amazing that it would even be necessary to make this the first principle for contemporary church renewal. Yet the fact remains that the message of personal salvation is not going forth consistently in the church. During the last fifteen years I have rarely, if ever, heard laypersons testify to hearing a call to personal commitment to Christ. I realize that many of them sat under such preaching without it making a conscious impression,

---

[159]Outler, *John Wesley*, 197.

[160]*Enthusiasm* was a negative term in the eighteenth century, roughly synonymous with our term *fanaticism*.

but the whole matter cannot be written off that easily. Too many churches have settled into a moralistic view of Christianity that is fundamentally humanistic rather than Christocentric. The emphasis is on being good and doing good, but with little emphasis on the power to accomplish this kind of living. In this respect we are not unlike the sleepy Anglicans whom Wesley sought to awaken.[161] We can be sure that John Wesley would do all within his power to advance the preaching of personal faith in Christ.

Second, Wesley would urge Christians to *greater degrees of discipline.* In a very real sense, his whole life was an example of Christian discipline. The parsonage years at Epworth grounded him in the fundamentals of discipline. The Oxford years, especially after 1725, served only to give further shape to his disciplined life. In Georgia, Wesley maintained a pace that would have broken most men. His diary records that for over sixty years Wesley lived a remarkably disciplined life.

In 1778, Wesley preached an interesting sermon titled "The Work of God in North America." It was his attempt to relate the various dispensations of divine providence in the American colonies as far back as 1736. In the sermon Wesley commented on the preaching of George Whitefield, which has been acknowledged as a contributing factor to the first Great Awakening in America. Wesley noted that on Whitefield's last journey to America the evangelist lamented that many had drawn back unto perdition. In a telling statement Wesley sought to account for their decline:

> And what wonder? For it was a true saying, which was common in the ancient church, "The soul and the body

---

[161]One of Wesley's most effective sermons was titled "Awake, Thou That Sleepest." Cf. Jackson, *Works,* 5:25–36.

make a man; and the spirit and discipline make a
Christian." But those who were more or less affected by
Mr. Whitefield's preaching had no discipline at all. They
had no shadow of discipline; nothing of the kind. They
were formed into no societies. They had no Christian connection with each other, nor were ever taught to watch
over each other's souls. So that if they fell into lukewarm-
ness, or even into sin, he had none to lift him up. He
might fall lower and lower, yea, into hell, if he would; for
who regarded it?[162]

Hardly any quotation from Wesley is more insightful than
this one; it clearly shows his feeling about the necessity for discipline in the Christian life. Yet, this attitude can be easily misunderstood in our time when "hang loose" and "chill out" have
come to replace "shape up" as a guiding principle. Three facts
need to be mentioned to enforce and interpret Wesley's idea.

The first is theological. Discipline is essential because of
humanity's bent to sinning. If we are left to ourselves to merely
"do our own thing" and "go with the flow," we will shun the
disciplined life. Christian maturity is not automatic; it must be
cultivated. Discipline is the means of this cultivation.

Second, Wesley's insistence on discipline must not be viewed
in a narrow, legalistic, or even cultic sense. It is too easy (and
wrong) to read into these remarks the demands of a spiritual
dictator who required a set course of action from his followers. It
must be remembered that Wesley spoke of discipline first in terms
of principles. The rules for the united societies are based on principles Wesley believed to be scriptural and in keeping with the
practices of the early church. To a large extent, he left the partic-
ularization of those principles up to the various societies. The
specific disciplines he recommended were those that had been

162Jackson, *Works,* 7:411 (sermon: "The Work of God in North America").

well tested in the history of the church. His was no novel or faddish approach to discipline. It is important to see Wesley's views as those of a benevolent spiritual director who knew the basic principles and best expressions of the disciplined life.

Third, Wesley's discipline was all-encompassing. He did not major in minors or get hung up in the minutiae of the disciplined life. The goal for Wesley was holiness, which he called "the fulness of faith." The outcome was not this or that particular expression, but rather the renewal of the image of God.[163] In order for this transformation to take place, Wesley knew that nothing less than the consecration of one's entire self to God would suffice. He trusted the individual, in cooperation with the Holy Spirit, to work out the specifics of that consecration. When Wesley's commitment to discipline is seen in this light, it is clear why such a spirit must be at the heart of any significant renewal today.

With regard to Wesley's third key action in his strategy for renewal, he would urge believers to *get together in groups*. It was by proclamation that Wesley sought to extend the kingdom; by the societies he sought to mature it. These twin activities formed the heart of early Methodist evangelism. As the years went by, Wesley began to observe some deterioration in the group structure, and he warned against it in the strongest terms:

> Never omit meeting your Class or Band; never absent yourself from any public meeting. These are the very sinews of our Society; and whatever weakens or tends to weaken our regard for these, or our exactness in attending them, strikes at the very root of our community. . . . The private weekly meetings for prayer, examination, and particular exhortation has been the greatest means of

---

[163]Outler, *John Wesley*, 28.

keeping and confirming every blessing that was received
by the word preached and diffusing it to others. . . . Without this religious connection and intercourse the most
ardent attempts, by mere preaching, have proved no last-
ing use.[164]

In terms of contemporary church growth, Wesley was ahead
of his time in realizing the potential in group ministries. However, he was only drawing on the resources of a principle that
went back to the earliest Christian church.[165] A fruitful study
awaits anyone who will examine Wesley's bands, classes, and
societies in a search for contemporary connections and relationship to small group dynamics.

How can we square this emphasis of Wesley's with the many
churches in the Wesleyan tradition that limit corporate ministries to church school and public worship? We cannot. The
lack of relational ministries in the church has contributed
significantly to a loss of spiritual vitality. God has not designed
that the members of the church should function individually.
Dependence, mutual responsibility, and corporate nurture are at
the heart of what it means to be the church. To be sure, group
experiences can become perfunctory, and they surely have their
own set of problems. But to omit them from the ongoing life of
the body of Christ is to work against time-honored patterns of
renewal and to lose the Wesleyan spirit in this important area.

Fourth, Wesley would call us to a *renewed appreciation for
the sacraments.* As previously shown, he saw sacraments as
divinely instituted means for conveying grace to people. His
views on both baptism and the Lord's Supper clearly raised
them above the level of mere symbols and gave them a potency

---

[164]Jackson, *Works,* 11:433.
[165]See Acts 2:46; 5:42; Romans 16:5.

to effect changes in the lives of people.[166] Baptism (while not identical with new birth or regeneration) did convey grace to cleanse a person of the guilt of original sin and infuse a principle of grace "which will not be wholly taken away unless we quench the Holy Spirit of God by long continued wickedness."[167] The Lord's Supper was ordained of God to convey "either preventing, or justifying, or sanctifying grace, according to (our) several necessities."[168]

The sacraments were an important way for people to continually remember the objectivity of Christianity. It is of *grace,* not of ourselves that we are what we are. The sacraments were constant reminders of this truth. Because early Methodism did stress personal experience (conversion, assurance, sanctification, and so forth), it was all the more important to keep this objective balance before the people.

We may be sure that Wesley would call us to sacramental renewal and to a new vision of the power of these means of grace. He would call us to be present on all occasions when the sacraments are administered, especially Communion. He would urge congregations to administer the Lord's Supper frequently.[169] He would want us to believe that God desires to bring about renewal through the sacraments today, just as throughout the ages of church history.

Fifth, Wesley would urge that *Christ be offered to everyone.* Wesley never let the Methodist movement become his only concern. He constantly kept the needs of the larger church and the nation at heart. He believed that Methodism was one way

---

[166]Two representative treatises are "On Baptism" (*Works*, 10:188–201) and "The Duty of Constant Communion" (*Works*, 7:147–57).

[167]Jackson, *Works*, 10:192.

[168]Jackson, *Works*, 1:280.

[169]Evidence from early Methodism seems to suggest at least a weekly observance of the Lord's Supper.

God had chosen to bring a cure to the sickness of society. The varied ministries of the Foundry in London illustrate his concern for the whole gospel. There he carried on a full-orbed preaching and discipling ministry, operated a medical dispensary, ran a bookstore, organized a school for children, and provided a shelter for widows (one of whom was his mother). He had a particular concern for the poor, feeling that the English aristocracy had abandoned them.[170] There is no doubt that he would exhort us never to forget that the world is still our parish.

In our own time the cause of social concerns goes under many names and grows out of differing philosophies. It is important to understand Wesley's social contribution in light of the ideologies that promote social reform today. The key for doing so is the recollection that Wesley's social concern was inextricably rooted in the Christian faith. He was fundamentally an earnest Christian who sought through a variety of means to effect the redemption of fallen humanity.[171] For this reason Wesley cannot be used as a support for Communism, Marxism, or any other "ism" that has at its heart an atheistic presupposition. Nothing in his social concern can be identified with destructive or violent expressions of revolution espoused by any contemporary movement. His was the power of love and compassion working *within* a society that had its share of injustices.

The testimony of some historians that the Wesleyan revival was the greatest force for social change in the eighteenth century is a testimony to the legitimacy of *Christian* methods to evoke transformation. It calls into question any movement that divorces itself from a Christian motif and acts as though the end justifies

---

170See Maldwyn Edwards, *John Wesley and the Eighteenth Century: A Study of His Social and Political Influence* (London: Epworth, 1955).

171See chapter 7 in Henry Bett, *The Spirit of Methodism* (London: Epworth, 1937).

the means. Wesley would call us to a ministry to the total person in the total society—all over the world. But he would always stress the need for such ministry to be distinctively related to the name and spirit of Christ.

Obviously these are only some of the principles for renewal exemplified in the life and ministry of John Wesley. I am convinced that these principles are timeless. They stand at the heart of authentic Christianity, ancient or modern. If we use the term *Methodist* in any sense comparable to the way Wesley used it, we cannot ignore these principles. If we do ignore them, though we may still call ourselves Methodists, our founding father would not know us. If we apply them, God will bless us and give life to that portion of his body known as Methodism.

Questions for Reflection and Discussion

1. Which of the renewal strategies mentioned in this chapter seem to be most important for your church? Why?
2. What expressions of lay ministry do you have in your church?
3. How can the church today call people to discipline without falling prey to a legalistic spirit?
4. What values do you see in having another Christian or group of Christians with whom you can share your experience?

For Further Reading

Hunter, George. *The Contagious Congregation*. Nashville: Abingdon, 1979.

Outler, Albert. *Evangelism in the Wesleyan Spirit*. Nashville: Tidings, 1971.

Snyder, Howard. *The Radical Wesley and Patterns for Church Renewal*. Downers Grove, Ill.: InterVarsity Press, 1980.

Chapter Twelve

TO SERVE
THE PRESENT AGE

*Wesley's primary concern was for the realization of
God's dream in every person and in our world.*

PAUL CHILCOTE

A new century evokes fresh explorations. This is true in theology as much as in any other area of life. As the twentieth century turned into the twenty-first, articles and books of all kinds appeared, seeking to understand the present and future in relation to the past. New conversations have debated the proper blending of "tradition" and "openness." Within the Christian community, much has been said about the evolution from modernity to postmodernity.[172]

Although some of the topics would be foreign to John Wesley, he would be right at home in talking about a time of transition. The eighteenth century was itself a "time between the times." Agriculture was giving way to industry, and the notion of private ownership was exerting a powerful influence on British society and politics. As with any "gap time," people were falling through the cracks, and there was a wider division than usual between the prosperous and the impoverished. Wesley saw clearly the need to deal with this cultural change and the application of the gospel to it.

Thanks to Charles Wesley, the early Methodists sang their way right into the middle of their age with these words:

> To serve the present age,
> my calling to fulfill:
> O may it all my powers engage
> to do my Master's will![173]

---

[172]I use these terms cautiously and without any specific definitions—only to acknowledge the sense of change that pervades our time.
[173]Charles Wesley, "A Charge to Keep."

The spirit of the people called Methodists is still the spirit of Christians in the Wesleyan tradition today. We have no other age to serve but the one we're in, and we recognize it to be one of substantial and radical evolution. As we come to the end of this book, we will explore the relevance of the gospel for the time in which we live. This chapter serves as a kind of reprise in relation to what has preceded it. It aims to shift our focus from the past and cast our vision toward the future. Wesley helps us in making this transition.

First, Wesley's understanding of theology reveals an awareness that *the gospel always leads us to truth larger than the age in which we live.* Wesley was a citizen of the eighteenth century and a "Church of England man." But his mission was to advance what he so often called "scriptural Christianity." Rather than allowing culture to shape his message, he strove to see this gospel influence the culture. His theological content and his ministry system were grounded in the Bible, with a strong doctrine of grace underlying the whole thing.[174] Running through his sermons, treatises, letters, and journal is an explicit and implicit superstructure of Scripture. He never apologized for the fact that who he was and what he did was shaped by the Word.

In particular, Wesley found a solid foundation in the writings of the early church—the period from the close of the New Testament (c. A.D. 90) to the middle of the fifth century (c. A.D. 450). Not only was this a time different from his own, but he saw it as a foundational era for the development of the theology of the church—development that took place over a long period of time, in widely different cultures, and under the leadership

---

[174]Wesley's understanding of "scriptural Christianity" with the keynote of grace must not be viewed as limited to the New Testament. We have already seen his desire for the Methodists to be shaped by "the whole counsel of God," and that brings the Old Testament message to bear on his theology and ecclesiology as well.

of numerous leaders—including significant church councils and other communal efforts. It was a period of time when the biblical message was interpreted and expressed both in the church and in the society. However, Wesley's appreciation did not lead him to attempt a return to the past.[175] On the contrary, it served as the superstructure for a theology developed precisely to address the time and place in which he lived.

In a postmodern era when we strive to be liberated from captivity to a particular time and a single culture, we can learn from Wesley as an example of one who sought the same thing in his lifetime. Robert Neville has described both the challenge and the tension in such a quest: "The process needs to resist the siren calls for simplicity that usually result in either losing the gospel in the excitements of culture or adopting a historic expression of the gospel that addresses some other culture than the one that is our mission field."[176] Wesley would agree with these words, and as we study his life and work we discover how to engage our generation fully, doing so with timeless biblical authority and contextualized cultural sensitivity.

Second, we serve the present age by *being more concerned about people than ideas.* As we've seen, John Wesley was a "life theologian" more than a propositional one. He believed the prosperous were called to be stewards of God's provision, and he felt the poor to be the particular objects of God's compassion and concern. He saw how materialism had made the rich proud and self-centered, and he lamented how the downtrodden were often left in confusion and without hope. He could not imagine

---

[175]It is true that for a while (c. 1727–35) he gave greater weight to "primitive Christianity" than he did in later years, even flirting with it as an ideal era. But thankfully this caricature did not remain, but only the abiding sense that the early church was in some ways "foundational" for subsequent history.

[176]Cited in Neal F. Fisher, ed., *Truth and Tradition* (Nashville: Abingdon, 1995), 40.

any proclamation of the gospel that did not address life as people were living it.

He backed up his words with a whole system of caregiving that included ministry in schools and orphanages, medical care, literacy training, and many other forms of neighborly compassion. The offerings taken in the societies were not primarily to keep the wheels of Methodism turning, but they were to be used to relieve suffering. When he spoke of "practical divinity," he included within it a sociology of religion, not merely a theology of religion. He used the power of his pen to try to influence England's ethic as much as its faith—never defining spirituality in purely intangible ways. The way to heaven included not random acts of kindness, but a conscientious and continuous application of the gospel to life.

In this regard, we cannot fail to note a significant (but often overlooked) element in Wesley's methodology. He permitted membership in the united societies *before* conversion! The requirement for membership was "a desire to flee the wrath to come," and this was precisely a connection to prevenient grace, not converting grace. Wesley's understanding of transformation began with the association of non-Christians with Christians. He believed that one of the best evangelistic strategies was to get unconverted people into fellowship with converted ones so that they could receive their love, hear their testimonies, and have questions answered by those whose experience of Christ was genuine.

Unlike some Christian communities where conversion was a requirement for fellowship, Wesley took the more radical approach. But it was an approach rooted in his absolute confidence in the power of the gospel to achieve its end—the salvation of souls. As subsequent studies of early Methodism have shown, most of the actual conversions to Christ through the Methodist movement occurred from six weeks to six months after a person began participating in the meetings—after their hunger for God was guided into a transforming experience of God in Christ.

Our postmodern age places a high premium on experience. We can learn from Wesley's willingness to run the risk of including "experience" along with Scripture, tradition, and reason in his theological method. He was clear in his belief in the Bible as the inspired Word of God, and he resolutely affirmed the historic creeds of the Christian faith. But he understood that Christianity is more a life to be lived than a creed to be espoused. Perhaps the greatest confirmation of this fact took place at the time of his funeral. Wesley had intentionally planned the service to be very early in the morning so as to avoid a crowd—or so he thought. But early as it was (5:00 A.M.), it is estimated that 5,000 people turned out to bid farewell to one whom they knew had loved them to the end.

Albert Outler recognized the experiential strength in Wesley's theology when he wrote, "John Wesley was the most important Anglican theologian of the eighteenth century because of his distinctive composite answer to the age-old question as to 'the nature of the Christian life': its origins, growth, imperatives, social impact, final end."[177] In this statement Outler captured the core of Wesley's life and work, recognizing that he could never rest until what people believed came to saturate the way they lived. For Wesley, the gospel life was nothing other than fulfilling the two great commandments—love God and love neighbor.

---

[177]Albert C. Outler, "The Place of Wesley in the Christian Tradition," in *The Place of Wesley in the Christian Tradition*, edited by Kenneth E. Rowe (Metuchen, N.J.: Scarecrow, 1976), 14.

We continue to serve the present age as we place formation above information. This in no way minimizes or reduces the need for biblical content in theology or the need to develop sound doctrine, but it means that the test of theology's influence is Christlikeness and the holy living (for example, the fruit of the Spirit) that expresses it. Paradoxically, no creed or dogma has to suffer in the hands of a good life theologian. Rather, "dead orthodoxy" will become "living faith" when approached in this way.

Third, Wesley helps us through the example of his *eclectic approach to truth*. He was rooted in the Anglican tradition, but he did not limit his search for truth and his communication of it to that single source. An examination of his sources reveals a direct connection to Roman Catholicism, Eastern Orthodoxy, classical Protestantism, Puritan, and independent sources. He drew from these various streams because of the obvious overlap of ideas between and among them. But beyond that, he looked for ways to connect the traditions, believing that such a synthesis was both true to the gospel and contributive to a stronger faith than would be possible from any single thread.

This eclectic spirit never violated Wesley's basic orthodoxy, but it did result in a message that kept ideas in a dynamic union rather than separating them into a competing posture. Paul Chilcote has rightly noted that one of the key words in Wesley's theology is *and*. For example, Wesley developed a theology of faith *and* works, yet he avoided dividing the two, which he believed would result in a weakening of the gospel and lead to the extremes of quietism on the one hand and works-righteousness on the other.

What emerges is an ecumenical orthodoxy of the kind found in the historic creeds, councils, and confessions. In our contemporary quest for truth, we can take guidance and confidence from the notion that truth can be found in many places. We can emerge with a larger and richer view of the body of Christ. The result does not have to be an unbounded pluralism (as is sometimes the case in contemporary theology), but it can be the very "catholic spirit" Wesley espoused in his day and that unites the whole people of God in ours.

Fourth, serving the present age means *keeping the world as our parish*. The gospel always propels us beyond ourselves. Even the deepest personal holiness evaporates unless it is expressed in social holiness. To be sure, the world has changed dramatically since the eighteenth century, but Wesley's heart for all people everywhere is surely akin to what we want to see in our day. In the Wesleyan covenant service, we express the fact that "Christ has many services to be done." There simply is no one way, or better way, to make Christ known. On the contrary, we must search for those places and ways where the Holy Spirit has preceded us to create "ports of entry" for the gospel and the temporal and eternal benefits it brings.

Wesley represented this sentiment through such things as direct evangelism to the masses, literacy efforts (educating girls as well as boys), medical care for the sick, establishing homes for orphans and widows, and relief to the poor. His experience in Georgia had showed him the need for a global presence of the church. And the last letter he ever wrote—a letter to William Wilberforce—revealed his own desire to see slavery abolished. It is impossible to understand the gospel or the ministries that flow from it apart from a global presence and societal influence.

We would be hard-pressed to find a more significant connection between Wesley and us than this. We live globally as much as we do locally. Wesley's example keeps the world ever before us, but not in a way that enables us to overlook those closest at hand. Furthermore, he challenges a postmodern choice-oriented culture by reminding us that we cannot limit the gospel to any particular cause or concern. Disciples span the spectrum of service, making room for people to use their gifts and graces in a wide variety of ministries that lead to regeneration, renewal, and reform.

We are called to serve the present age precisely because it is the only age in which we have the opportunity to live. In a very real sense, the only kind of Christian we can be is a "contemporary Christian." But we learn from Wesley that this never means we live in isolation from the faith tradition and cultural evolution that have brought us to our time and place. Rather, it means taking a constructive approach, using the building blocks given us by our past and arranging them in ways that speak to the world today.

Years ago, Dr. William Quick made a statement in our seminary chapel that I have never forgotten—a statement that speaks to the spirit of serving the present age with all the resources of the past at our disposal. He said, "A generation which forgets those who came before it deserves to be forgotten by those who come after it." Here is the reason we have used the pages of this book to explore the way to heaven. We will not be in heaven by ourselves, and we cannot get there in isolation from those who precede and follow us. To the extent that we keep this view alive in our theology and our ministry we will create a view of the gospel that is both respectful of our ancestors and worthy of attention by those who carry on the gospel after we're gone.

Questions for Reflection and Discussion

1. Which of the lessons from Wesley strikes you as being the most important to pay attention to in your life or in the life of the church? Why is this so?

2. How have you found the little word *and* to be important in the shaping of your own faith?

3. What would you like to pass on as your legacy to those who will carry on the gospel after you're gone?

For Further Reading

It is almost impossible to list either primary or secondary materials for this chapter. The bibliography beginning on page 155 will give you a number of resources to use in further grasping the way to heaven and your living it out in the world today. It is unfortunate that many good books don't stay in print as long as they should. I have made an effort to list resources that are available at the time this new edition is published. As a means to extend the spirit of this chapter, however, I highlight three books that can especially strengthen your desire to serve the present age:

Chilcote, Paul W., ed. *The Wesleyan Tradition: A Paradigm for Renewal.* Nashville: Abingdon, 2002.

Job, Rueben P. *A Wesleyan Spiritual Reader.* Nashville: Abingdon, 1997.

Weems, Lovett H., Jr. *Leadership in the Wesleyan Spirit.* Nashville: Abingdon, 1999.

A Basic
Bibliography for
Wesley Studies

This book is a primer in Wesley studies. Consequently, I'm approaching the bibliography in the same spirit. I have not assumed any previous knowledge of the Wesleyan tradition in this book or in the list that follows. Instead, I have listed relatively few resources to extend your study—materials either still in print or comparatively easy to find. Most of the works cited have their own bibliographies, thus enabling you to go even farther in your reading.

Primary Material

Baker, Frank, ed. *The Bicentennial Edition of Wesley's Works*. The early volumes were published by Oxford University Press, but the remainder have been published by Abingdon Press. Each volume has its own editor. The late Frank Baker was the general editor for the series. This is surely the definitive edition of Wesley's works, even though it will be some time before all of the thirty-four intended volumes are available.

Curnock, Nehemiah, ed. *The Journal of John Wesley*. London: Epworth, 1938, 8 vols. This is the standard edition of Wesley's journal. It also contains Curnock's transcription of Wesley's unpublished diaries.

Jackson, Thomas, ed. *The Works of John Wesley*. Grand Rapids: Baker, 1979, reprint edition, 14 vols. This is the best available set of Wesley's works. Until the bicentennial edition is completed, it will remain the major resource for studying Wesley.

Sugden, E. H., ed. *The Standard Sermons of John Wesley*. London: Epworth, 1956, 2 vols. Sugden's annotations are helpful in giving a fuller understanding of the sermons Wesley selected to serve as doctrinal standards for Methodism.

Telford, John, ed. *The Letters of John Wesley.* London: Epworth, 1931, 8 vols. Until the volumes of letters in the bicentennial editor are completed, this edition will continue to be the best source for studying Wesley's correspondence.

Wesley, John. *Explanatory Notes Upon the New Testament.* Grand Rapids: Baker, 1987, reprint edition. These notes, together with the standard sermons and articles of religion, comprise the historic doctrinal standards of Methodism.

——————. *Explanatory Notes Upon the Old Testament.* Salem, Ohio: Schmul, 1975, reprint edition. This set completed Wesley's attempt to provide inexpensive annotated versions of the Scriptures for the early Methodists.

SECONDARY MATERIAL

Ayling, Stanley. *John Wesley.* Cleveland: William Collins Publishers, 1979. A fine biography written by one who is not Methodist, so in some places he lacks the familiarity with Wesley's thoughts that others would reveal.

Chilcote, Paul W. *She Offered Them Christ: The Legacy of Women Preachers in Early Methodism.* Nashville: Abingdon, 1993. This volume explores the significant contributions of women in early Methodism. It is already considered a standard source for this topic.

Chilcote, Paul W., ed. *The Wesleyan Tradition: A Paradigm for Renewal.* Nashville: Abingdon, 2002. This volume, with contributions from Wesley scholars whose doctrinal studies were funded in part by A Foundation for Theological Education, is one of the finest one-volume explorations of how the historic Wesleyan tradition can guide the church in the twenty-first century.

Collins, Kenneth J. *The Scripture Way of Salvation: The Heart of John Wesley's Theology.* Nashville: Abingdon, 1998. On a more scholarly level, this book develops Wesley's theology as an "order of salvation" in ways unique to this volume.

Demaray, Donald E., ed. *The Daily Wesley.* Anderson, Ind.: Bristol House, 1994. An excellent anthology of key themes in Wesley's writing, paraphrased by Dr. Demaray in an accurate and readable fashion. It's an excellent way to become familiar with Wesley's own words and ideas.

Harper, Steve. *Devotional Life in the Wesleyan Tradition: A Workbook.* Nashville: Upper Room, 1995. This book highlights the place of spirituality in the early Methodist movement and gives detail about the societies, classes, and bands—as well as the instituted and prudential means of grace.

Harper, Steve. *Prayer and Devotional Life for United Methodists.* Nashville: Abingdon, 1999. Although the title makes the book appear to be limited to one denomination, it is actually devoted to a more in-depth examination of the role of prayer and spiritual formation in the Wesleyan tradition.

Hunter, George G., III. *To Spread the Power.* Nashville: Abingdon, 1987. This book remains the finest exposition of Wesley's mission, particularly as it expressed elements found in the contemporary church-growth movement.

Job, Rueben P. *A Wesleyan Spiritual Reader.* Nashville: Abingdon, 1997. Using a prayer-book format, Bishop Job has arranged writings from Wesley into six months' worth of devotional readings. Job's introductions to each week's theme are an added jewel that you can actually use in your daily devotions.

Kinghorn, Kenneth Cain. *The Gospel of Grace.* Nashville: Abingdon, 1992. Here is another excellent summary of the gospel according to Wesley, with a particular focus on the doctrine of grace that runs through it. Kinghorn's appendixes are as valuable as the text itself, supplying the reader with one of the most extensive listings of Scripture references, hymn citations, and bibliographic resources in any single place.

Maddox, Randy. *Responsible Grace: John Wesley's Practical Theology.* Nashville: Kingswood Books, 1994. This book seeks to provide a reflective overview of John Wesley's characteristic theological activities and convictions, with a special emphasis on the practical-theological dynamics of Wesley's work as theologian. An excellent and accessible resource for studying Wesley and his theology.

McKenna, David L. *What a Time to Be Wesleyan! Proclaiming the Holiness Message with Passion and Purpose.* Kansas City, Mo.: Beacon Hill, 1999. A good example of a contemporary Wesleyan writer who effectively interprets Wesleyan theology in our time, particularly the doctrine of holiness. If this doctrine has seemed stodgy or lifeless to you, you're in for a treat as you read this book.

Oden, Thomas C. *John Wesley's Scriptural Christianity: A Plain Exposition of His Teaching on Christian Doctrine.* Grand Rapids: Zondervan, 1994. This book combines choice extracts from Wesley's own writing with the observations of the author, who is himself an esteemed Wesleyan scholar. The result is a work that connects the past and the present in the Wesleyan tradition for the edification of believers and the church.

Outler, Albert. *John Wesley.* New York: Oxford University Press, 1964. Nearly forty years after its original publication, this volume remains a standard anthology, giving the reader both seminal extracts from Wesley's pen and among the best introductions about Wesley from Outler's pen.

Runyan, Theodore. *The New Creation: John Wesley's Theology Today.* Nashville: Abingdon, 1998. Standing somewhere between a purely popular and a scholarly book, Runyan succeeds quite well in giving a substantive look at Wesleyan theology and its application for today.

Snyder, Howard. *The Radical Wesley and Patterns for Church Renewal.* Downers Grove, Ill.: InterVarsity Press, 1980. This volume remains one of the best examinations of Wesley's vision and his methods for implementing that vision.

Tuttle, Robert. *John Wesley: His Life and Theology.* Grand Rapids: Zondervan, 1978. This book, written as though Wesley himself were speaking, remains one of the few books that can provide a very accurate understanding of Wesley, while doing so in a most appealing style. It has been an effective resource to make Wesley come alive to readers who have never encountered him before.

Weems, Lovett H., Jr. *Leadership in the Wesleyan Spirit.* Nashville: Abingdon, 1999. This book provides a good overview of Wesley's life and work as it helps inform and guide Christian leadership in the church today.

Williams, Colin W. *John Wesley's Theology Today: A Study of the Wesleylan Tradition in the Light of Current Theological Dialogue.* Nashville: Abingdon, 1960. This volume remains one of the finest interpretations of Wesley's theology, with the added value of showing how Wesley's thought connects with and advances ecumenical Christianity.

Yrigoyen, Charles, Jr. *John Wesley: Holiness of Heart and Life.* Nashville: Abingdon, 1999. This book may be the best introduction to Wesley's doctrine of holiness. It is written in a very readable style by one of the premier Methodist historians of our time.

We want to hear from you. Please send your comments about this book to us in care of zreview@zondervan.com. Thank you.

ZONDERVAN.com/
AUTHORTRACKER
follow your favorite authors